# CLOSE TO COLETTE

# CLOSE TO COLETTE

*AN INTIMATE PORTRAIT*
*OF*
*A WOMAN OF GENIUS*

By

Maurice Goudeket

WITH AN INTRODUCTION BY

Harold Nicolson

*NEW YORK*
FARRAR, STRAUS AND CUDAHY
1957

© 1957 by Farrar, Straus & Cudahy, Inc.

The introduction by Harold Nicolson is reproduced
by permission of *The Observer*, London.

Library of Congress catalog card number 57-6766

Manufactured in the United States of America
American Book–Stratford Press, Inc., New York

# INTRODUCTION

COLETTE herself wrote many autobiographical studies, of which the happiest are those which recall her childhood at Saint Sauveur, and the most tragic, such as *Mes Apprentissages* and *L'envers du Music-Hall,* those which describe the eight years of married life with Willy or the six years when she earned her living by capering like a faun upon the variety stage. It was not till 1910, with the immense success of *L'ingénue Libertine* and *La Vagabonde,* that she achieved eminence as a writer of unusual originality and strength. From then onwards her fame spread throughout the Old World and the New, culminating in an apotheosis, when her poor old body lay in state encircled by flags and guards of honour and the people of Paris in their thousands followed her coffin to the grave.

It was in 1925, when staying with friends in the South of France, that she first met Maurice Goudeket, her third husband. She was fifty-two years old at the time and he was thirty-five. They remained inseparable until the day of her death, thirty years later. "It was hand in hand," he writes, "that we made that long journey together. . . . Every moment was a moment of fulfilment and silent happiness." For him, she was an incessant adventure, constantly rediscovered and renewed: for her, he was the devoted companion, bringing security, confidence and calm.

In this grateful and affectionate memoir, Maurice Goudeket emphasises those sides of Colette's character which were not always apparent to the outside world. To the casual visitor, I am assured, she seemed a formidable and intimidating figure; with her penetrating sapphire eyes, her deep grumbling voice, and her Burgundian accent in which the R's rutilated like kettledrums. He shows us her gentleness, her dignity, her zest, her self-discipline, her simplicity, and her hatred of pose.

She retained her romantic and her vagabond elements, and would read Victorian travel books in which women explorers penetrated to remotest Africa in button boots. But essentially she was domestic, a typical housewife of the French middle class. She enjoyed her linen cupboard as much as her books: she knew all about how to cook truffles, to preserve apricots, or to make orange wine. She detested anything that seemed squalid, untidy or Bohemian and insisted always that a successful marriage must be based on mutual respect and that the lubricant of such a relationship must be conjugal courtesy. She detested scenes or passionate embraces: when in 1941 Maurice Goudeket was arrested by the Gestapo and marched away to some unknown destination, she did not indulge in hysterics. She merely tapped him on the shoulder in an affectionate manner and uttered the words "Off you go!" Yet when some friends heard shrieks of laughter coming from their sitting-room and inquired what the joke had been about, she replied: "Nothing at all!

It was just that he was with me and I was with him!" No
wonder their marriage was so successful.

He was entranced by her childish simplicity; for him she
was often just the little country girl from Saint Sauveur who
knew all about mushrooms, loved garlic, and sprinkled salt
upon her bread and butter. When they were invited as dis-
tinguished guests on the maiden voyage of the liner *Normandie,* she arrived with a basket containing a cold chicken,
several hard-boiled eggs and a game pie, in case they ran
short of provisions on the way. Her love of nature was in-
fantile in its simplicity; she would say that it was not our
business to inquire into what went on in a forest; she would
leave crumbs for the mice in hotel bedrooms; and, even as a
very old woman, would stretch out her arms in ecstasy when
alone with the smell and murmurs of a wood. Her understanding of animals was that of some primitive being, she
would talk to them in a special language and knew all about
their hypocrisy and sense of sin.

As a writer, she was immensely conscientious, resolved
always, even when most rushed and overworked, to write
nothing below her own standard. Her attitude towards her
work was practical and humble; she was submissive when in-
trusive people asked her for prefaces or to inscribe their
copies of her books. "Her kindness," writes Maurice Goudeket, "to ordinary people arose from the fact that she did not
regard them as ordinary." Her essential innocence, as the
atrocious Willy once observed, "resembled that of a native
of Tahiti in the days before the missionaries arrived."

I am sure you will enjoy this entrancing portrait, often
amusing, often deeply moving, of a woman of genius and
courage.

HAROLD NICOLSON

# CLOSE TO COLETTE

# I

IN THE ROOM where I am writing, nothing has changed. On the chimney-piece there are the Chinese crystal balls. The armchairs are there, adorned with strips of tapestry which she worked with her own hands. Behind me, above the books and surmounting a niche, there is a head in plaster by the sculptor Saint-Marceaux, which followed her in all her removals. Practically nothing which has been acquired since we have known each other. I had taken up my abode just as I was, in her surroundings, happy to forget my preferences in order to adopt hers. The work that I did to spread the knowledge of her writing has hardly changed either: correspondence with publishers all over the world, with producers and students and interested people. Nothing has changed except that I shall never get over the impulse which draws me into the next room.

How difficult it is to discriminate between what one wants to tell and what one wants to keep to oneself. Does not the whole value of memories lie in their secret, in the fact that

3

they are shared with no one? There is a great temptation to consider that the intimate hours of a person or a couple, whatever their public position may be, belong to themselves alone. But when a wave of fervour such as has rarely been seen irradiated the last years of Colette, bearing her in the end to that high catafalque aglow with the colours of the tricolour, and when that murmur of love which shows no signs of abating has been one's surest consolation, would it be fair not to offer in exchange the most precious thing one has kept? Thinking of her, too, what can I do for her henceforth except serve her work, and how can I serve that work other than by illuminating it through what I know of her person, troubled only by my powerlessness to show her in her true greatness? I shall keep for myself nothing of her that should endure, and when the moment comes, I will take you with me into the room which, at the end, she hardly ever left, into her own enchanted place where every object was for her a symbol and a wonder perpetually renewed.

I shall not be much help to her future biographers concerning what happened before my time. The fact is that she and I lived together in the most natural way. That was what made our happiness. If I had not completely forgotten, in our daily behaviour, that I was concerned with an extraordinary person, our relations would have acquired a sort of constraint which both of us would have disliked. Not only did I never take a note of anything that she may have said to me, but, for fear of playing the part of a biographer in spite of myself, I dare say I questioned Colette less about the past than it is normal for a husband or even a friend to do.

Whenever we try to evoke a particular moment in the life of someone who has disappeared, all the aspects under which we have known that person are present too. Let no one be astonished to find here an apparent disorder, and strange measurements of time. Memory has its own requirements; it is too lively a thing to be controlled, and any other order but its own would be arbitrary.

Only yesterday we were living like any woman with any man. Sometimes we talked of work, hers or mine, but just as a carpenter and his wife talk of their work-bench and the orders they have to execute. Alone in my room I would bend over one of her books with the same enjoyment as any ordinary reader. My love for the woman and my admiration for her work ran as it were parallel.

However much we may love a person and be loved by him, he constantly eludes us, but as long as he is there we are reassured. To-day I search for Colette not only in my memory and my heart's memory, but in her books where there is always the glorious chance of finding her on every page. Because she never described anything that she had not observed, and because she considered creatures and things directly, without any preconceived idea, no works have better reflected their author. How could I henceforth separate them? I am not so ungrateful to destiny as not to value at its true worth the privilege of such a link with what I have lost.

My infatuation was no recent thing. I was fifteen or sixteen years old when I discovered Colette, and received from that first reading of her a delicious shock. With the incredible pride and fanciful notions of that age, I said to my parents: "I am going to marry that woman. She is the only one who will be able to understand me."

I am not priding myself on that as though it were a prophecy. Out of the countless desires we formulate, if one or other of them bears fruit, we call it premonition.

# II

I<small>T HAPPENED</small> in the house of some society people where I
quite often used to dine, and where I had made the acquaintance of Marguerite Moréno. One evening, without
my having been warned, as I entered the drawing-room I
saw Colette there; she had been brought by her great friend
Moréno. She was lying flat on her stomach on a sofa, dressed
in a printed frock. With her head raised under its crown of
dishevelled hair, and her bare arms, whose beautiful modelling at the shoulders struck me as a bit too plump, she looked
like a large cat stretching itself. I had never met her, never
heard that bronze voice of hers, rolling its Burgundian r's.
Why it was I do not know, but I observed her without
charity. At table I found that I was placed on her right. I
remember that Léon Blum was there too. Hardly had she
sat down than Colette seized an apple from a basket of fruit
placed in front of her and bit hungrily into it. I thought that
she was playing the part of herself and my suspicion increased: but I could not take my eyes off that most indi-
vidual profile of hers, with the eye set so expressively in the
shadow of a lock of ash blonde hair, the nose rather long at

its end, the wide cheek-bones, the thin bow of the mouth and the pointed chin. I poured her out a drink and she looked astonished and shot me a look blue as night, ironical and quizzical but with an indefinable nostalgia in it too. Something countrified and healthy emanated from her.

I uttered a few banalities, and she replied with a naturalness which once again I took for an attitude. She took no part in the conversation which was bandying general ideas across the table, except once, with a "Why?" which challenged all that had been said, embarrassed the speakers and produced no answer. The rest of the evening dragged. She did not enjoy herself much. Neither did I. I did not see her again until a month later, and then briefly in the corridors of the Théatre de la Renaissance, where she was playing Léa.

Easter fell early that year, 1925. I made a plan to spend a few days in Italy, then gave it up for no reason. I had no particular interest in anything and very much had the feeling that I was at a dead end. I had always expected too much of fate without doing anything to help it. As a matter of fact I had never learnt how to pass from a madly imaginative childhood, fed by literature, to a more realistic youth and maturity. When I was a child I dreamt of glory, but of glory as a thing in itself, without even an idea as to how I could win it. As for love, that would only occur when I met, in the most romantic circumstances, a marvellous being with whom I should remain until we died together on the summits of ecstasy and passion.

By the time I was thirty-five I had still not sobered down much, so in order not to betray this childish state of mind I behaved with the greatest circumspection, which made me appear cold and formal, not quite at ease. When I did occasionally form an attachment I would break it off at once, because I wanted to keep myself with all my emotions intact for that unique love in which, at the bottom of my heart, I no longer believed. I brought out a little volume of poems which won some approval, but that was not what I meant by glory and so I stopped, if not writing, at least publishing anything. A certain success in business brought me comfortable circumstances, but above all boredom. It was no good telling myself that to ask of fate what it cannot give you is to run the risk of drying up, and that to refuse what life offers is to chance not recognising happiness if it comes your way. I had got set in my habits and withdrew further every day.

In the end I decided on Cap-d'Ail and that hotel, now transformed into flats, where the friends whom I had in common with Marguerite Moréno were staying. We travelled down in my car, Marguerite, a young man whom we were to drop at Nice, my chauffeur and I. The car was open, the cold belated. We had to stop from time to time to unfreeze the people sitting behind. Marguerite was wearing the cloak, made out of an old rug, that everyone always remembers her in. She sparkled with humour the whole way.

We had been several days at Cap-d'Ail, all among the beds of mauve wallflowers, when Marguerite announced to us that Colette was arriving the next day. This arrival had not been planned by the two friends. But Moréno's nephew who had remained in Paris was anxious to rejoin his aunt. And as Colette had just acquired a new little car, he had pointed out to her that the only way to break in a car was to take it as far as Cap-d'Ail.

—"Oh!" said I, "and we were so peaceful!"

My friends looked at me and I listened to the echo of my own words within myself. There is no doubt that the memory of my first meeting with Colette made me feel uncomfortable every time I thought of it. She had made a strong impression on me, and that was enough to put me on my guard, so used was I to restraining my inclinations.

She came. During the day she remained invisible, going out, and working. In the evening we all gathered for dinner and afterwards played at a harmless game of cards called *"taminti,"* short for *"t'as menti"* ("you lied"). Colette used to laugh heartily at it, giving full rein to her vivacity and gaiety. But I became more and more reserved, so much so that one of the players, since the game consists of discovering who is lying, remarked: "It's difficult with Maurice. He's always as calm as . . . as . . . ." Colette threw me a quick glance over the cards and completed the comparison: "As a covered flame," she said, to my astonishment.

The next day I received a telegram recalling me to Paris, and I decided to leave that evening by the train. In any case all of us were more or less about to depart. Colette's car, driven by Pierre Moréno, had already started on the return journey to complete its breaking in. I offered Colette mine, which otherwise would have returned empty with the chauffeur. She accepted joyfully, since she liked nothing better than dawdling along by road.

I said good-bye and went off to wait for the Blue Train at Monte Carlo. On the way I thought over the past few days with a shade of regret, but also with relief. After all it was neither possible nor desirable that there should be anything between her and me. A letter of thanks, a book with an inscription, and there our relations would end. It was best that it should be so.

I had not reserved my place, but I travelled frequently at that period and I knew that it was always possible, in those days at any rate, to come to some arrangement with the higher-ups of the *Wagons-lits*. If the worse came to the worst the attendants used to keep for themselves a compartment over the wheels which they were always ready to give up. In short there never had been an occasion, however great the crowd, when I had not been able to find a place on the night train. But on that particular day I did not succeed. No matter how charming I tried to be, using all the arguments which I thought decisive and backing them up beyond what is normal, there really was not a spare corner. So there was nothing for it but to return, rather crestfallen, to Cap-d'Ail.

I said to Colette: "I gave you that car so that you could travel back to Paris in it and I couldn't take it away from you. But now it's my turn to ask you for a place in it, which you can refuse if you like." She began to laugh. We left the next morning.

What can I say of that journey? I drove, Colette sat beside me and the bored chauffeur was at the back with the luggage. We crossed a Provence all pink with peach-trees in flower, on our way to meet those more variegated springs of Burgundy and the Ile de France. Colette talked little but when she did she brought the whole countryside into the car, the very nature of the soil, the deep scent of all growing things, the invisible bird, the hidden water.

During lunch she put a question to me: "Why do you write?" and that led me on to talk a bit about myself. How accessible she was, how clear and simple everything became when one was with her! At a word or a phrase from her I felt all my inhibitions leaving me one after another, and I no longer even dared to call them by that barbarous name. For the world which she restored to me was a real world, the world of everyday poetry, which was to become our dwelling-place.

When I got back to Paris I received a book. It was *La Vagabonde,* inscribed "for Maurice Goudeket, in memory of a thousand miles of vagabondage." An invitation to lunch accompanied this gift.

I sometimes think how much the shaping of a destiny and the binding of a couple together depend on successful meetings and the avoidance of snares. A door which one thought was closed, a watch that is slow, a false step, a traffic jam, a sleeping car available . . . and your fate is settled. Let others trust in the stars if they like to sort out these entanglements; if ever I believe in a God I shall have too lofty an idea of him to involve him in such gropings of the blind. We walk across a cemetery of happinesses missed for lack of a word, a gesture, an airy bubble; and how many people, meant for each other, have passed each other by in the fog?

# III

THERE WERE NEVER any more beautiful eyes in the world, nor any which knew better how to see. They were blue, of a blue which changed according to the light, as do all blue eyes, but a deep blue, blue like certain sapphires, blue as the Mediterranean in winter when the mistral torments it, and lightly specked with gold. They were in truth sea-coloured. There was at one time—perhaps it still exists—a club for people with sea-coloured eyes, which had appointed her its president. Visitors always agreed that none of her photographs, no snapshot or painting, ever gave any idea of the alternating intensity and sweetness of her gaze. When she turned it upon a stranger he would immediately feel himself sized up at his true worth and fall silent or begin to stammer. If he was bold enough to speak to her of those eyes, she would answer him: "It is just that I know what to put into them." For I never heard her reply to a compliment other than by disparaging herself.

She used to put kohl on her eyes with a little stump which, several times a day, with a very sure movement, she slid along inside the eyelid from one end to the other. But I knew her look without the kohl: it was only a shade lighter.

She thought that this would preserve her eyes. Her sight became weak quite early; she was astigmatic, and in addition her left eye lacked a third of the ordinary field of vision. For all that her sight never varied during the whole time that I knew her and perhaps it was to the kohl that she owed this.

Sometimes she used to point out to me in the distance a bird, a dog or a cat that I could hardly make out, naming them by their species or race. "I recognize them by their style," she would tell me.

It is not only with one's eyes that one sees; there are piercing glances which see very little.

She was a product of the French soil at its purest, French to her finger tips, and a provincial above all. She loved moving house, but it was so that she might immediately build another nest and establish her province there. She was a provincial in her art of living, her household recipes, her tidy cupboards, her provisions, her punctuality, her proverbs, her boxwood and lily of the valley, her Twelfth-cake, her mulled wine, wood fires, chestnuts and slow bakings under the ashes.

She was both home-loving and adventurous, in the way that cats are, passionately attached to what she possessed and ready to risk or give it away at any moment. Ready to undertake the craziest of schemes, and begin a career all over again. Gay but not optimistic, and so quick in her gestures, thoughts and decisions that it was difficult to follow her. Her love of the marvellous made her credulous and inclined to agree with the first opinion uttered, though nothing could modify her profound nature. I used to say to her: "You are credulous but you cannot be influenced."

She was timid, uncertain of herself, and so little convinced of her merits, so modest in short that it was almost an inferiority complex. Because of this she was sometimes abrupt, raising her voice and indulging in sudden outbursts. She resembled her brothers, both in what she has told us of Achille and by what I knew of Léo. The first impulse of her half-brother Achille, the doctor, when he heard a patient ring at the door, was to jump out of the ground-floor window and hide in the garden.

Léo, the younger, a surprising person all of a piece, had made for himself a life according to his choice, a modest life, but which he would not have exchanged for any other in the world. A clerk in the office of a lawyer in the suburbs of Paris, with a very modest salary, he lived for fifty years in the same sixth-floor room. The efforts which Colette and I sometimes made to better that existence only met with refusals because what we called comforts he described as complications. All he liked was stamps, billiards, classical music and statistics. He was never known to have any sentimental attachment. He was not even unsociable, so sure was he of preserving his independence; he was absolutely impregnable.

But above all he remained wholly turned towards his childhood. That garden of Sido's to which Colette returned little by little, Léo had never left. He knew the faintest of its scents and still heard the creaking of the gates; he climbed the trees and wandered about the village. Colette has related how he would come to dinner with us without ever announcing himself and often after long absences, tall and dried-up, holding himself very straight, with his high forehead, his regular features, his drooping moustache, and on his nose a pince-nez of the most old-fashioned kind, ever-lastingly humming or whistling between his teeth. Without any introduction, unless it was to sit down at the piano and play Chopin with unpractised fingers but a very gentle touch, he would begin to talk of what he called "down there." Colette would enter into the game and it was won-derful to hear them competing by memory, first one and then the other quoting something, correcting a detail and walking about in their childhood with steps which never hesitated.

They were an astonishing family to have come out of a village of thirteen hundred inhabitants, as Léo would have said, for he knew by heart the number of "souls" in most localities, the dictionary being one of his favourite books. It is true that neither Sido nor the Captain was a villager, since she was born in Paris and he came from Toulon. But originality so authentic, and such independence of judgment, would be a subject of admiration in no matter what family. All musicians into the bargain.

How full and satisfying must have been that life in com-mon at Saint-Sauveur, under the wing of the incomparable Sido—we know the Captain less well—to have remained in the minds of the children as a lost paradise which shaped them forever afterwards.

She was sincere when she used to declare that if circum-stances had not led her to write, she would never have done so all her life long. There may well never have been a writer with less of a vocation to write, and as soon as one knew her well one ceased to be astonished at this. It is true to say that the vocation to write springs from the need to express things which would otherwise remain in you unfulfilled, unsatisfied, and turned inward, the need to clarify your thought, occasionally to enthuse and often also to endow yourself in imagination with what life refuses you. A desire for celebrity, and a particular flattering celebrity at that, is rarely absent from it.

Colette lived so intensely, her curiosity and her enthusiasm found such sustenance in the smallest living creatures and even objects, and in the care which each demanded, that to live was for her occupation enough in itself. Extremely active and always on the go, until such time as arthritis immobilised her, in her eyes no occupation was superior or inferior. A manual trade would have given her the greatest pleasure. It was not a more noble activity to write than, for example, to make a pair of sabots. Each needed to be performed as well as possible, with care and attention to detail. In general she never classified things and beings in order of merit, considering that they deserved equal attention for different reasons.

But just because she considered writing as a task, and because she had all the virtues of the French artisan—humility, patience, self-exaction, pleasure in a well-finished article—she never let a page leave her hands of which she could have thought: "That will do well enough." She always wrote as well as she possibly could, and thus it happened that she produced an immense body of work where you could search in vain for ten lines which do not contain some image full of savour, some penetrating notation. She was like a provincial violin-maker who, unknown to himself, was making instruments worthy of a Stradivarius.

The word inspiration seemed to her one of the most suspect in the French language; exaltation was hardly better.
But when she was writing Colette used sometimes to con-
centrate so hard that she would gradually get colder and
colder. She put rug after rug on her knees and shawl after
shawl on her back. When she was finishing a book her ap-
plication became such that one had the impression she was
really giving of her substance, as a bee gives its honey. Capable at such times of working eight or ten hours at a stretch,
she used in the end to look like a cocoon. Whether she
liked it or not she was not far at such times from a sort of
trance-like state. Let anyone re-read the last paragraph of
*La Naissance du Jour,* describing the dawn, and tell me if
the final sentence does not give the impression of a text inspired rather than thought out:

"The cold blue has crept into my bedroom, trailing with
it a very faint tinge of flesh colour that clouds it. It is the
dawn, wrested from the night, drenched and drawn. The
same hour tomorrow will find me cutting the first grapes of
the vintage. The day after tomorrow, even before this hour,
I want . . . Not so fast! Not so fast! That deep hunger for
the moment that gives birth to the day must learn patience:
the ambiguous friend who leaped through the window is
wandering  still. He did not put off his shape as he touched
the ground. He has not had enough time to perfect himself.
But I have only to assist him and lo! he turns stall-keepers,
spindrift, meteors, an open and limitless book, clusters of
grapes, a ship, an oasis. . . ."

Her way of making contact with things was through all
her senses. It was not enough for her to look at them, she
had to sniff and taste them. When she went into a garden

she did not know, I would say to her: "I suppose you are going to eat it, as usual." And it was extraordinary to see her setting to work, full of haste and eagerness, as if there were no more urgent task than getting to know this garden. She separated the sepals of flowers, examined them, smelled them for a long time, crumpled the leaves, chewed them, licked the poisonous berries and the deadly mushrooms, pondering intensely over everything she had smelt and tasted. Insects received almost the same treatment: they were felt and listened to and questioned. She attracted bees and wasps, letting them alight on her hands and scratching their backs. "They like that," she would claim.

When at last she left the garden, she would pick up her scarf, hat, slippers, stockings, dog and husband, which she had shed one after the other. With her nose and her forehead covered with yellow pollen, her hair in disorder and full of twigs, a bump here and a scratch there, her face innocent of powder and her neck moist, stumbling along out of breath, she was just like a bacchante after libations.

At Saint-Tropez, in the height of the summer, great hornets sometimes streaked across the garden, metallic blueblack and very fearsome-looking. Louise, our caretaker, or perhaps it was Madame Lamponi, pronounced Lammpauni, had said: "They don't sting, those don't," but this remark left Colette unconvinced. She was not satisfied until she had managed to get hold of one of these insects and teased it to such an extent that thereafter she knew it had a sting, and a very cruel sting at that. Its prick, a most painful affair, left a little bump on her first finger for ever after. But she knew, and that was the main thing.

Among the senses she gave first place to the sense of

smell. "It is the most noble," she used to say, "the only one that never lets itself be abused, and allows of no compromise."

She absolutely had to know the name of anything she was contemplating, whether animate or inanimate, and if this name was unfamiliar to her, or escaped her, she never could rest until she had found it. This was not so much to store it in her memory, but because the name completed the identity of the thing in question, and was inseparable from it. She has sometimes been reproached for using difficult words, especially for flowers, plants and sea-creatures. The point is that for her they were not difficult words. Very often they belonged to quite common flowers and animals. Colette could never understand how anyone could be near them every day and not be anxious to know what their names were.

All the same, she had to give up the word *conferve* (silk-weed). It must be admitted that it is an impossible word. No matter how you pronounce it, it sounds like *conserve* lisped, and still less can you print it, for proofreaders untiringly correct it.

She even loved certain words for themselves, quite apart from the idea which they represent. She loved them for their music, but still more for their graphic aspect, their design. Has she not spoken somewhere of the letter S "standing on end like a protecting serpent"? During periods of intense work she would dream of words. "I've had a typographical dream," she sometimes said to me in the morning. Words and lines had danced a ballet specially composed for her. When a journalist from *Le Figaro* asked her if she was in favour of simplified spelling, she answered: "I don't want to have my words spoiled."

So even if she had never written a line, her attitude to things, because of her need to know them—in themselves and in their relation to the rest of the sentient world—to know them, define them and name them, was none the less essentially that of a writer.

# IV

I HAVE JUST come back from Brussels where Jean Cocteau, elected to the chair left vacant by Colette, was received by his peers. When he rose to pronounce the eulogy of Colette in the same place where, twenty years before, she herself had been received, I had once again the impression I have felt so often since her death, of a confusion in time. Twenty years before, in that same hall, I was sitting in the same place, and she who then rose and stood, dressed all in black, before an audience just as attentive, was receiving the first of the great honours which marked the last year of her life. The session yesterday was still intended to honour her and it was hard to persuade myself that she was not there.

Jean Cocteau had been my fellow pupil at Condorcet when we were both twelve or thirteen. Behind the man standing there, with his halo of grey hair beginning to recede from the high forehead above an arched nose in a face seamed with fine wrinkles, his long hands with their marked sinews fluttering ahead of his thoughts, I could see again a laughing child with his hair sleeked down. Moreover, Jean had been, in the last fifteen years of Colette's life, our dearest friend. We used to look forward to his visits, and they always took place at the most unlikely moments. He would arrive bringing with him the invisible cortège of his familiar myths. We loved his gaiety, his gentleness, his clear voice, and the nimbleness of his mind was a refreshment for us. With him there was hardly any need to speak. Every word between us carried distant echoes, subtle harmonies.

And there he is evoking Colette in her very movement, in the tone and turn of her phrases and, by associating himself and me with the scenes he is recalling, restoring to me exactly as they were, through every one of my senses, the hours that seemed dead and gone. It does not seem possible that the malicious child whose hair used to lie on his forehead like two little paint-brushes splayed out, the phantom of my youthful self, dreamy and uncertain, and the woman whose voice of bronze still echoes within the walls of this hall, carrying on its faint burr of enchanted words, should be at once so present, and forever absent. I have always held the conviction, as deeply rooted as an ardent faith, that there could be no such thing as an after-world made to man's measure, and for his benefit. But still less can I admit the idea of time imposed on us by our understanding, with a past accomplished for ever and a future empty of all events. It is enough for me to know in the depths of my being that Time, as we reckon it, is merely an imposture, for me not to feel really separated from my dead.

As a writer, Colette still awaits discovery, even for me. I have not been able to stand far enough away from her work, any more than anyone else has. In certain respects I have been less able to, since it was under my eyes that she wrote. It may be that she shows herself at her most astonishing in her chronicles, her occasional articles jotted down in haste. There are still quantities of these waiting to be brought out. I have some which she thrust aside contemptuously, suppressing them as being unworthy of a place in her completed works. When I was sorting them this morning, ready to agree with her decisions, my eyes fell unintentionally on a few sentences and I stopped my tidying. Here is one of them, about Yvonne de Bray, in a piece concerning Jean Cocteau's *Les Monstres Sacrés,* written for *Paris-Soir* whose messenger was waiting in the kitchen, as he often did, until he could "carry off the goods" at top speed to that machine for making a hash of words which we call a newspaper:

"Since yesterday the idea of metamorphosis has become linked with her destiny, and more than one spectator, as he watched that tall actress, swathed in a magnificent frock of flame-blue, pressing her two hands against her waist as though to raise her body out of itself, thought, as I did, of the final release of the dragon-fly from the pool, as it breaks out of its last sheath and gazes around with its bulging eyes measuring, as it reflects the universe, the evil and the good that it will be able to scatter there."

("L'idée de métamorphose est liée, depuis hier, à son destin, et plus d'un spectateur, en voyant cette comédienne à la haute stature, étreinte par une magnifique robe d'un bleu de flamme, appuyer les deux mains à sa taille comme pour se hisser hors d'elle-même, songea, comme moi, à la dernière éclosion de la libellule des étangs qui crève son dernier fourreau, projette autour d'elle le regard de ses yeux bombés et mesure, en reflétant l'univers, le mal et le bien qu'elle y pourra répandre.")

There, solidly based on Latin—which Colette did not understand—we have a beautiful sentence in the French tongue. Test its balance and equilibrium. It is the grand sentence of the seventeenth century with its parenthetical clauses, its suspense, its rhythmic march and finally its rich and ample close. It is the sentence of Pascal, of Bossuet, and of those sacred orators with whom Colette was not familiar. Later on, only Chateaubriand . . . but it was only in the very last years that I made Colette read the *Mémoires D'Outre-Tombe*. It is a very virile sentence, which doubtless no man could have written, because he would have left out the detail of the dress, and the gesture of the actress.

If anyone asks me to explain, from what I know of her, why a former little village-girl, with nothing but her elementary school certificate, wrote, as it flowed from her pen, the language of the gods, if the gods are French, I shall speak of her gift of observation, I shall plead her musical sense, her perfect ear, without satisfying anybody, and certainly not myself. If Colette had been asked, she would perhaps have answered what, in that same article, she wrote of the art of Cocteau: "The art of Cocteau is neither more simple nor more explicable than are the solar spectrum, the folding-up of the sensitive plant, a child's crime, or the movement of some minute sea-creature which, far from the sea, still obeys the rhythm of its native tides."

Although she dwelt at such length on the paradise of her childhood, how little she spoke of herself in spite of appearances! For the thirty odd years that she spent in Paris before I knew her, I am more or less reduced, as I have explained, to the same sources as the ordinary reader: a silhouette in *La Vagabonde,* very little in *L'Entrave* and hardly more in *Mes Apprentissages.* On her life as a woman, silence. But I can form a judgment on her legend, because the essential character of a being does not vary, hers less than anyone's. I shall not make the mistake of presenting her as a model of all the virtues, as our common morality has codified them. That would be to betray her. If she had remained in the shadow of that stultifying bundle of rules, instead of the work drenched with truth which she produced, perhaps she would have become like that vinegary woman-commentator, right thinking but thinking little, who devoted to Colette throughout her whole life, and particularly after her death, articles laced with diluted poison.

It did not seem to Colette so easy to distinguish between good and evil. It has been thought she loved scandal. It was merely that she had personal ideas about what is scandalous, what is or is not honourable conduct, what is worthy of esteem or even of attention. As she was not given to sparing herself, was incapable of precaution or hypocrisy, and frank into the bargain, she sometimes asked for trouble.

Free as she was in speech, I shall astonish many people when I say that no one could have been more modest. "You forget that at one time she danced naked." In the first place it was a nakedness limited, for better or worse, to the showing of one breast for which, in addition, she had no need to blush. Besides, to say that shows a total unawareness of how isolated from the public the footlights make one feel. And whenever she took up a job, she thought it was not decent to refuse anything that the job demanded. Moreover, with her, modesty, like her other austerities, was only the result of her natural propensity. She was amoral, if you like, in so far as morality is a code which is taught. But her quick sense of honour, which was valid for no one but herself, her refusal to take the easy way, her severity towards herself took the place of rules for her. She used to say "One must be careful not to fall in the direction in which one naturally leans."

# V

"YOU ADORE BRITTANY, and from now on you'll love the South." Every man has a tendency to lure a woman away from a past in which he has not shared, and to offer her new skies like a present to welcome her. But I limited my tyrannical instincts to such changes of scene as this. Even with someone less strongly and definitely organised than she, I do not think I should have acted otherwise. How many men are never satisfied until they have imposed upon their companion all their own ways of seeing and feeling! They think that by this means they will make sure of their domination over her. But they forget that they will be the first to tire of finding before them only a pale reflection of themselves, of hearing nothing but an echo of their own voices.

She and I always realised that daily happiness necessitates daily vigilance. An expression she often used was "conjugal courtesy"; this in her view excludes slovenliness and demands in the first place that the married couple should spare no efforts to remain for each other, at all times, as attractive as possible, even after passionate love has given place to more lasting sentiments. Those who are not afraid of noisy yawns or bellowed songs, grimaces in the mirror, and sloppy bedroom slippers, will answer: "What does it matter so long as you love each other?" Colette thought on the contrary that care for one's appearance and a certain constraint also, in the man as well as the woman, assure the moral hygiene of a couple and its durability, as in the case of that English Civil Servant who, having spent twenty years alone with a few natives in a lost corner of Nepal, only avoided going mad by putting on his dinner jacket every evening until nothing remained of it but a few rags.

There was a news item which she had also kept in mind. A woman in England, after thirty years of marriage, had killed her husband, without being able or willing to say why. Finally, pressed by questions, she admitted that for years it had been torture for her to sit down at table with him, because of the noise he made when drinking his soup. One day, able to bear it no longer, she had assassinated him. She was hanged; Colette swore she would have let her off.

We were never afraid, she and I, to touch on the subject of that separation which in one way or another awaited us one day. We were agreed that suffering is not in itself an honourable state and that there is no need to bear any of it that you can avoid. "I do not like people who scratch their wounds," she used to say. We claimed that one had the right to choose between living and dying, but that having chosen life, it was an offence to it to give it a poor welcome.

How vain it is to speak of grief before you experience it! However lucid we may be about our feelings and our passions, it is no more possible to project them into the future than to imagine, for example, hunger when you are satiated, or satiety while you are hungry. No sooner have you decided that sadness is merely indulgence in self-pity, than you realise, when you lose a beloved person, that it is not really a question of sadness.

During the two months which, after my arrest, I passed in the camp of Compiègne, she covered Paris with a network of telephone calls, knocking tirelessly at every door where she hoped for help. Apart from that she kept up a good countenance, neglecting neither her work nor the care of her person or her household. But she would rise at night, go to my room, sit at my work-table and remain there for long hours, motionless. How could I surpass in courage one who had more of it than anyone in the world?

# VI

IT IS NOT enough to say that she loved animals. Before every manifestation of life, animal or vegetable, she felt a respect which resembled religious fervour. At the same time she was always aware of the unity of creation in the infinite diversity of its forms.

One evening she gave me a striking example of this. We were at the cinema, watching one of those shorts which show germinations accomplished in a moment, unfolding of petals which look like a struggle, a dramatic dehiscence. Colette was beside herself. Gripping my arm, her voice hoarse and her lips trembling, she kept on saying with the intensity of a pythoness: "There is only one creature! D'you hear, Maurice, there is only *one* creature."

Whether it were man, animal or vegetable, the most urgent thing for her was to help. Goodness can be nothing but a general feeling of tenderness for everything. Hers sought first to be useful; it was active, rough if need be, and sometimes aggressive. While she was still living in the Boulevard Suchet, wagons with worn-out horses harnessed to them often passed by late in the evening. Sometimes she heard their drivers, more or less drunk, striking their animals. She would quickly slip on a dressing-gown, go down in the empty night, march straight up to the aggressor, exchange insult for insult with him and not let him go until she had cowed him. One day she managed to make an impression on a particularly tough brute by saying to him: "You mark my words, it won't be long before you die and in the next life it'll be your turn to be the horse." Against all her expectations she saw him lower his head and make off murmuring "think o' that!" full of fear and contrition.

Once when a discussion had taken her rather far from her house and she was returning about two in the morning along the ill-lit boulevard, another danger awaited her. Two very evil-looking men came up alongside her and, each taking an arm, one of them said, dragging his words: "Well, my little lady, so you're not afraid of the dark?" "No," she replied in a quiet voice, "since I've got two toughs to look after me." No doubt they had never met a woman so sure of herself. Whatever it was, they left her in front of her door.

She never left any animal indifferent. They knew at once that, from an animal point of view, they were dealing with someone considerable. That knowledge generally expressed itself by a spontaneous sympathy, but sometimes also by hostility. Colette was not offended by this, understanding and respecting this antagonism and not trying to make the animal change its feelings.

Two animals were involved in our life, the bulldog bitch Souci, and the Cat. I deliberately use the expression "involved," which will not astonish those many persons who consider animals other than as ornamental or useful objects.

Animals in a household can be, like children, a cause of discord as well as a link. I confess that dogs leave me rather cold. I treat them well, I'm "polite" with them, but they have no place in my heart. Their barking—especially that of other people's dogs—irritates me in the highest degree and as for all that business of lifting legs and sniffing behinds, I don't understand it. For the cat tribe on the other hand, I feel a boundless tenderness, so that if I never considered Souci other than as Colette's dog, we had the Cat in common. I even used to find myself saying "the Cat that we had together."

Colette, who was not much given to hierarchies where humans are concerned, always put the cat before the dog. A dog has friends only but a cat has its enemies, who almost all feel for it a physical aversion, and its worshippers. It is useless to expatiate on their merits since nothing will convince the former and the others have had their minds made up long since.

Colette made herself perfectly understood by her animals. Without ever raising her voice, she obtained from them what was sometimes absolutely against their nature. Having said to the Cat in a certain manner: "Cat! Once and for all you are forbidden to touch the finches," the Cat quivered and lay down with her paws tucked in, content thenceforward to watch the finches dreamily, closing her eyes from time to time, the better to resist the giddiness of temptation.

The bitch Souci, a little French bulldog, was black and white with pouches under her eyes and a black snout. Though a bit of a liar by nature, she lied badly. Colette had only to say to her: "I hear what you're thinking" and the bitch would confess, lower her head, and take refuge on the little tub-chair which had been given over to her. On other occasions, having some piece of mischief in view, she took to limping, which gave her away at once.

Colette used to address animals politely, speaking French to them and not baby-talk.

We had bought the Cat at a cat-show in the Avenue de Wagram, or rather, as Colette said, it was she who had bought us. Surrounded by her fellows, all of them uneasy and agitated, there she was in her cage, a grey chartreuse, four months old, with short thick fur and yellow eyes, perfect in shape and as fresh as a rose, sitting motionless, wise and composed. She was so touching that some people who had realised that Colette and I were putting our heads together, came up to us and begged: "Buy her, buy her, Madame Colette."

We decided to carry her off on the spot as though she were a fiancée. As my car was an open one I began to fuss about a basket, a collar and a leash. "What for?" said Colette. "She knows already that she is mine."

We tried out some ambitious names for her, Tahiti for instance, because grey pearls come from Tahiti, but she only wanted to be called "The Cat," "as though there were only one in the world."

She figures literarily in *La Naissance du jour* and other works. She is not only the model of the feline character in *The Cat,* but what was more, that book would not have been written without her. Dead, and not replaced, she became in *L'Etoile Vesper* and elsewhere "The Last Cat."

It was to her that Colette and I used to apply those lines
by Musset:

> *Et le moins que j'en pourrais dire*
> *Si je l'essayais sur ma lyre*
> *La briserait comme un roseau.*

That is why I shall say no more about her.

What is normally referred to as "love of animals" has certainly nothing in common with the veritable connivance
which existed between them and Colette. And one might
say almost as much for the vegetable world. When she
busied herself over flowers it was not, as with the rest of
us, merely to keep them beautiful as long as possible. The
most important thing was to save and sustain life; it was a
question of pity and love:

"I dedicate to those imprisoned flowers a little of the
pity that I have for caged animals. Almost as much alive as
animals, flowers die more quickly from a journey, or when
they find a niggardly shifting soil, with no depth. As the
plant perishes one can measure how much life it had and
how much it clung to it. The way it weakens, the pathetic
drooping of its floral head, are just like an actual heart-
attack accompanied by pallor, since at those times the plant
suddenly shows the whiter underside of its petals and its
leaves. If water comes to its aid in time, it revives in the most
moving manner. How many moments have I not wasted—
but can I call them wasted?—in the company of flowers that
are great drinkers, like the anemone, the tulip, the hyacinth
and the wild orchid. Fainting with heat and thirst, once
they are plunged into water their stalks fill so richly and

greedily that one can actually see the energetic gestures by
which the flower returns to the vertical; jerkily at first and
then by a series of tremblings, when the head is too rich and
too heavy.

"What a tender pleasure it is for me to watch a tulip reviving in a crystal goblet! The ink dries on my pen, but
before me another work, interrupted by a momentary death,
is striving towards perfection and will attain it, shine for
a day and fade the day after . . . I do more than watch the
tulip regain its senses: I hear the iris unfolding. Its last pro-
tecting silk rustles and splits all down that azure finger
which itself unfurled only a moment ago, and if you happen to be alone in a little quiet room, it can give you quite
a start if you have forgotten that on a nearby table an iris
has suddenly decided to flower. Just think that in the Cours
la Reine there are thousands of irises flowering in constant
succession.* The earliest sunlight frees those whose time has
come and I begin to envy that moment when, in the light
of dawn filtering through the tent, I might hear the per-
ceptible sigh of so many irises all unfurling together."

What tenderness there is in that page! Is it not clear that
for Colette, the difference between an animal and a plant
is not so great? "There's only *one* creature."

She was like a corner of the French countryside, which
had been allowed to tell its own tale, to sing of itself, or
else like a radar which had received the gift of poetry.

A sorceress she was in the strict sense of the word, and
she never ceased to wonder at it. Other gifts of prophecy
also made her so. Some of her books appear to be relating

* An annual show of irises was formerly held in the Cours la Reine.

episodes of her life, although they actually preceded them. And when we were separated, it sometimes happened that her letters answered questions which I had not yet put to her.

# VII

S HE HAD never been in the South in summer. Those who braved its heat during the hottest part of the year were at that time only a minority: I was one of them. I had no trouble in persuading Colette to come and share a tiny little house called "La Bergerie," which I had rented at Guerrevieille, a hamlet on a hillside among pines on the Côte des Maures, near Beauvallon. Everything about Provence, as it lay under the summer sun, its bright colours, its pungent scents and even the stridency of its cicadas, captivated her from the outset like a rediscovered country. One must not forget that her father's family lived at Toulon and that he himself had been born in the district of Mourillon.

It was very hot when we arrived at Guerrevieille and we decided to put everything else aside and go down to bathe. The first step Colette took in the sea she trod on the spines of a sea-urchin. I was just about to remark to her that this was not a very practical way of catching them, when I saw that she was in great pain and could hardly stand. We had to go and see a doctor at Saint-Tropez, on the other side of the bay, so that he could pull out the spines one by one;

the sole of her foot was riddled with them. This was her first contact with the place where for the next fifteen years we spent all our holidays.

Saint-Tropez has been described too often for me to try my hand. At that time it was a lazy little port, whose rare summer visitors, chiefly painters, did not disturb its peaceful life. Yachts had not yet chased the decrepit local single-masted boats away from the harbour. Not a car on the quay-side. Empty barrels lay there awaiting a far-distant vintage. In the evenings, in the local bars the young people of the country would dance to the tunes of mechanical pianos, the boys with each other and the girls with each other.

Colette was enchanted. We could only stay at Guerre-vieille for fifteen days, after which she had to undertake a tour of casinos throughout France with the play *Chéri*. She immediately set people looking out for a peasant's house which she might buy in the neighbourhood of Saint-Tropez. The one we were told about, at the end of our stay, could not have been more modest. It consisted of four rooms, none of them big, and lacked every comfort. But adjoining the kitchen there was a little terrace, facing north, surrounded with a balustrade and covered with a heavy wistaria which gave shade at all hours of the day. But the little property—just over two-and-a-half acres, half of it planted with vines—included a garden, a little spinney of fir-trees, a few fig-trees and an inexhaustible well. But you only had to go through the vines and to cross the hill-road and a little deserted beach to get to the sea. But already Colette was peopling the garden mentally with shrubs and flowers, building here and demolishing there, and settling in.

The property was called "Tamaris les Pins." "A nice

name for a railway station," she said. Just as she was never able to begin a book until it first had a title, she wanted the property to have a name fit to use before she concluded the purchase. Round the well, near the entrance to the garden, there was an ancient vine whose grapes were apparently still excellent. "And they are muscats" remarked the proprietor with a tinge of respect. "Good," said Colette, whose decisions were almost prompt, "we'll call it 'La Treille Muscate.' "

Ah! those first few years of ours at Saint-Tropez, before the invasion of the coast came to spoil everything! The fulness and the savour of the days, divided into walks first thing in the morning, then gardening, bathing, the siesta and work. The nights, the scented nights, murmurous with the song of frogs, the chirping of crickets!

The little house was improved from year to year. We added on a room which provided a terrace for the first floor, a patio pierced with arcades which claimed to provide shade, but was chiefly an excuse for climbing plants, which incidentally were difficult to train, soon a new little room encroached on the terrace, and an outside staircase led from this room to the patio. A garage was built by the side of the Route des Salins, as far away as possible from the house, and on top of it a little room for the caretaker. A frigidaire replaced the old system of clinking bottles drawn from the bottom of the well; we lost in picturesqueness what we gained in comfort.

All these works, if they prolonged the cordial presence of the trade-guilds amongst us, never made the house beautiful or really comfortable. But so long as Colette inhabited it she magically created the illusion that it was. It is true that the little garden was smothered in flowers, that a great stretch of wall was covered with a thick tapestry of morning glory of a luminous blue, that the little crystal drinking troughs attached to the trees attracted the birds from all parts, and that the sole function of the sunflowers was to keep the goldfinches with us by virtue of their smooth black seeds.

Meridional grandiloquence gave a final touch of grandeur to these modest places. When I asked Lamponi, the caretaker, "Where is Madame?" she would reply, "In the park," when Colette was in the garden, "In the forest," if she happened to be lying with her pets in the minute fir-wood, "In the countryside" for anywhere else.

Colette sold "La Treille Muscate" in 1938. It was no longer possible to stay there. The little house was so accessible, so undefended, that Colette found journalists, intruders, visitors, and autograph-hunters hidden in the garden, waiting for her in the house, and coming up to her on the beach.

In 1942, as a result of a final difference of opinion with our temporary occupants, I travelled about France a certain amount, and passed several months at Saint-Tropez. I asked permission of its proprietors, some industrialists, to visit "La Treille Muscate," telling them that I was the husband of Colette. They gave me a good welcome: "Come in, Monsieur Willy," they said with a smile, proving that they were well read too.

I write this without irony. Monsieur Willy is one of Colette's characters, since he figures in her first books. It is consoling to realise that literary personages grow old less quickly than others. In the same way it often happened that

when Colette passed by with her last bitch Souci, someone
would murmur: "Look, there's Toby-Dog!" without being
aware that Toby-Dog would by then have been forty years
old which, for a dog . . .

I entered without undeceiving my hosts.

Alas! when the enchanter has gone, magic quits the scene.
The "park" had become a rather sad little garden, the
"forest" had lost its sacred-wood charm, and the "countryside," dotted with a few straggling peach-trees, was reduced
to a small vineyard rather badly kept.

We quickly made friends with the little group of painters
who haunted Saint-Tropez. André Dunoyer de Segonzac,
Luc-Albert Moreau and André Villeboeuf jointly owned a
very pretty house there, on a height near the Chapel of
Sainte-Anne. The violinist Hélène Jourdan-Morhange, the
critic Gignoux, and Thérèse Dorny, were their guests. We
used to meet at bathing time on the little beach in front of
"La Treille Muscate." Nora Vilker, now Nora Auric, and
some other close neighbours, joined us.

Having risen early, Colette would call her animals, who
ran up at once. First there was the cat's walk, limited to the
vineyard and the little wood, but enlivened with all a cat's
games, pretences and gallopings. The dog had a right to a
wider territory. Knowing that she must not leave the enclosure, the cat would sigh as she watched Colette and the
dog leave the garden and disappear along the coast road. It
was a narrow road, bordered with close-set hedges, over
which convolvus straggled. Some fig-trees gave it shade, proclaiming themselves from far off by their scent at once
sweet and overpowering. In the early morning the whole

road was scented, smelling of thyme, wild mint and turpen-
tine-tree, and sometimes cut grass. A little later I would go
to meet Colette.

As soon as we had had our breakfast together under the
shelter of the wistaria, Colette immediately began to garden.
She put the greatest energy into it. When she had finished
using the secateurs she would sit down on the ground and
begin scratching the earth with her hands. The dog and the
cat never left her side, and all three got drunk with the
sharp scent which rose from the humus, all equally busy
with essential secrets, to a knowledge of which I could not
pretend.

As a matter of fact my parents had been more of city-
dwellers than it is possible to imagine. My father would say
to my mother: "You don't look well to-day. I bet you've
been to the Bois de Boulogne again." His theory was that
trees absorb all the available oxygen from the air, leaving
us not enough to keep us alive. Having been brought up
with such opinions on country matters, in spite of my great
goodwill I was not very handy at garden work. I used to try
sometimes. I needed all the instruments and tools there
were in the house: rake, bill-hook, sickle, saw, spade, hoe,
dibble, it was a mere chance I didn't demand a plough. At
the end of a very short time I had cut a finger or injured a
nail and my efforts remained there.

Then it would be time to bathe. Colette always went
straight into the water even when it was very cold, as it used
to be after the mistral had blown. Very supple, she swam
with easy strokes, keeping slowly but steadily on. And then
we would stretch out in the sun. After all that, lunch on the
little shady terrace made up for the exertions of the morn-

ing. Colette prefaced it with a rub of garlic: a crust of bread
dipped in olive oil, lavishly rubbed in garlic and sprinkled
with coarse salt. Lunch consisted of Provençal dishes only:
green melons, *anchoïade, rascasse farcie, riz aux favouilles,
bouillabaisse, aïoli.* . . . Cooked garlic seasoned every dish
and in addition, throughout the whole meal, Colette ate raw
cloves of it as if they had been almonds. She had a keen liking for it, which doubtless had come down to her through
her father from a distant past.

After a short siesta, with every shutter in the house closed,
she would begin to work.

Only once did she allow herself to give advice to a be-
ginner on how to write a newspaper report. That advice
figures in the preface which she agreed to give Renée
Hamon for her book *Aux Iles de Lumière:*

"But I don't know what one ought to put in a book . . ."

"Neither do I, if you can believe it. I've merely got a few
little ideas about what's better left out. Paint nothing that
you've not seen. Look for a long time at what pleases you,
and longer still at what pains you. Try to be faithful to your
first impression. Have no faith in the 'rare word.' Don't
wear yourself out by lying. A lie develops imagination and
imagination is death to the reporter. Take notes . . . no,
don't take notes. Beware of 'flourishes,' beware of rushing
into poetry. Don't write your report when you are where
the event is happening, or it will seem unrecognisable to
you when you come back here. One doesn't write a love
story while one is making love. . . ."

In *La Naissance du Jour* she took good care not to do that
herself! What a strange book it is! It was begun in 1927, at
Saint-Tropez in the places that it describes, a thing which

in Colette's books is exceptional for she always saw even
landscapes better when she was some way away. If ever a
novel appears to be autobiographical, that one does. Everything is in it, "La Treille Muscate," the garden, the vineyard, the terrace, the sea, the animals. Our friends are
called by their real names. Colette puts herself into it, describing herself in minute detail. Never has she pushed self-
analysis so far. The transparent allusions to her past are
authentic. The letters of Sido reproduce those which Sido
wrote. The odours are those which still delight my nostrils,
I have known those blue nights, I hear the chirping of the
cicadas, I feel the buffeting of the wind, my hand lingers on
the warm wall. Everything is there, except that *La Naissance
du Jour* evokes the peace of the senses and a renunciation
of love, at the moment when Colette and I were living passionate hours together, elated by the heat, the light and the
perfume of Provencal summers.

The reserve which she invariably exercised when it was
a question of deep feelings is not the only cause. I feel sure
that she had indeed envisaged this renunciation. Less out of
wisdom, for she had a liking for risk, than out of a tendency
to put away from her what she most desired. She often hesitated between taking something and divesting herself of it,
between keeping a thing and pushing it aside. "The difficult
thing," she used to say, "is not to give but to refrain from
giving everything."

But above all let no one see in that a tendency to morti-
fication, unless we must admit that a certain Jansenism has
permeated the blood of every Frenchman, however free he
may be. Thank God, Colette was endowed with a solid ap-
petite for the good things of this world—incidentally, I do

not think that it is the lukewarm who renounce most readily
—and derived a frank pleasure from their possession. But at
the same time there was in her a secret austerity and later
on it was she who, before me, decided that the time had
come for the two of us to turn love into friendship.

Of all Colette's books, this is the one that I prefer. It
comes midway in her work and I see in it the flower of her
full maturity. Bathed in poetry and of unequalled density,
richness and eloquence, *La Naissance du Jour* narrowly
escaped becoming only one long lyric-offering from Colette
to her household gods. Having promised her publishers a
novel she felt—and it was a pity—she must introduce a story
into it. This one is slender. The character of Vial, in particular, is not very consistent. I was not the model for it, as has
been thought, nor could I have been. I recognised in Vial a
young antique-dealer of Saint-Tropez, but my presence prevented the portrait from being a good one. Colette only began to speak of me twenty years later, in *L'Etoile Vesper,*
under the wing of friendship.

Out of our relations with the painters of Saint-Tropez and
those hard-working holidays, there came two fine illustrated
volumes: *La Treille Muscate* by Dunoyer de Segonzac, with
a text written for the occasion, and *La Naissance du Jour,*
illustrated by Luc-Albert Moreau, which appeared four
years after the first edition. Each of them is considered to be
its illustrator's masterpiece. There is nothing surprising in
that. Rarely has there been a greater intimacy between the
illustrators of a book, the author and the places described.
Segonzac and Luc-Albert Moreau came whenever the fancy
took them, to work either in the garden, the wood or the

patio. The ways of the house were in no way altered for them. According to the hour of the day, Colette would be "pottering," as she used to say, in the garden, or writing with her nose to the wall, using the little shelf of a rustic desk which had made the journey by road from Brittany and was not exactly the better for it. One of the illustrations of *La Treille Muscate* shows her thus, from the back of course. Segonzac never made drawings or preparatory sketches but set to work directly on the copper with a sure and elegant stroke of the burin.

Often we used to keep our painters to lunch and their companions would come and join them. Sometimes we would all gather in the evening down by the port, or else go and dine in the forest of the Dom, at the inn of that name. It is there that they used to make the *poisson au coup de pied,* whose manner of cooking is described by Colette in one of the chapters of *La Treille Muscate.* If we wanted to have game before the shooting-season opened, we had to give warning forty-eight hours in advance so that the poachers would have time. Morals were easy going in Provence and the laws not harsh. As the inn had no telephone, one telephoned to the police station at Bormes, which would send a policeman to pass on the order about the unlawful partridges or hares. Unless it was the policeman himself who . . . But I should not like to cast suspicion upon so honourable a body. In any case to do so now would be against the law!

# VIII

WHAT USED TO puzzle visitors to Colette was a simplicity which did not seem to them natural, and a naturalness which seemed to them a snare.

Even when the greatest honours came to her, nothing could make her aware of the place she held. I would sometimes say to her: "You are the only one who does not know that you are Colette, and if you knew that you are Colette, no doubt you would not be Colette."

I never ventured to praise her without precaution. It made her ill-at-ease. Once I said to her that she was one of the greatest writers of all time. She looked at me out of the corner of a blue and sceptical eye, and said: "That would be known." She never really knew that it was known.

She was set on being just like everybody else. If a stranger or an interviewer tried to entice her on to what they considered heights of thought, she eluded them adroitly. The most they could get out of her was "I haven't got, I never have had any general ideas." I remember a South American woman journalist, author apparently of several large tomes, who claimed that she had come on purpose from her far-off

continent to gather "from the greatest living feminine personality" an opinion on the serious problems of the day
and on the future of civilisation and written thought. She
shook hands, sat down and, pencil in hand, began: "What
do you think, Madame, from the ethnological point of view,
of . . ."

"You have very beautiful eyes, my child," said the grave,
caressing voice of Colette.

"What, Madame? Oh! Yes . . . well, I was asking you, in
view of the profound confusion in which to-day we find . . ."

"And how wise of you to wear yellow; it's exactly right
with your complexion."

After a few more attempts the lady ended by letting herself be drawn into a conversation concerning the butterflies
of the Amazon, wild orchids, cooking, perhaps; in short
everything which might have provided a dazzling interview
for her if she had not been solely occupied in settling the
fate of the world. She went everywhere in Paris and related
her misadventure to anyone who would listen. "All she
could find to say to me was that I had beautiful eyes. To me
who have written five books, one of which won the . . ."

How well Colette resisted the temptation to prophesy
which with age and fame comes so easily to writers! "My
poetry is earthbound" she declared to reassure us, and perhaps to reassure herself. For I would not swear that, conscious sometimes that she had something extraordinary in
her, she did not experience what she called, referring to
someone else, "the melancholy of the elect."

She had an astonishing, and revealing, forehead; she knew
it and never would agree to show it. A huge domed fore-

head, like Beethoven's. No matter if the fashions changed, dragging the hair backwards, she always wore hers pulled forward on her forehead. "My monstrous forehead" she called it. But there was not only feminine coquetry in that, in her who used to declare: "No one can escape from his own envelope." She also said "The feminine face needs leafage."

None of her photographs shows this forehead, save one. On the occasion of her eightieth birthday, several well-known photographers came to the house. Already then Colette hardly ever quitted the sitting position on her bed, beside her window in the Palais Royal, so that these portraits do not differ much. They show a homely Colette, with her blue lantern, her raft (the name she gave her divan-bed), her pen-pot, all the working tools which she herself has named.

But there was an American called Penn who took a staggering photograph. When it appeared in *Vogue* I could not believe my eyes at the sight of it. It shows merely a head and shoulders, isolating Colette from her surroundings, from her legend, and setting her exposed before posterity. Her head, propped on a clenched fist, rises out of what looks like a mass of stuffs and furs because of Colette's half-sitting and half-lying position. The expression of the face is severe, strained, intense. The forehead is revealed practically bare, vast, significant, the forehead of a genius; it is a striking picture, but also a betrayal, a violation of the personality. It reveals everything that Colette desired to conceal and of which no doubt she was partly unaware in herself.

One cannot say the picture resembles her. It is without sex, whereas Colette remained feminine to her last breath.

The charm, the amiability, the tender irony which character-
ised her are absent from it. It is, in reality, the photograph of
*the other,* of the hidden being which each of us carries
within ourself, of the one who alone was able to write certain pages of Colette. Who are the demons, friendly to
photographers, who aided Mr. Penn? What foreknowledge
guided him? Perhaps he did not know Colette's works and
was seeing their author for the first time. I cannot believe
that chance alone helped him. A great portraitist—there are
very few of them—is a kind of diviner, who sees beyond re-
semblances.

A man does not love a woman for her genius: he loves her
in spite of her genius.

*La Naissance du Jour* appeared in 1928, but the first
book which Colette wrote under my eyes was *La Fin De
Chéri,* finished in 1926. A little drama, short but intense,
accompanied the publication of this book: it came out
shorn of thirty-two pages which formed a complete chapter.
It is difficult to imagine what that means for a writer. The
omission of this passage did not make the book totally in-
comprehensible, which would at least have attracted the attention of the reader: it merely made of it a badly balanced,
apparently slap-dash work, whose interest suddenly dropped
for lack of the explanations supplied by the omitted chapter.

For any writer worthy of the name a book is the product
of a slow and painful exudation into which each time he
puts the best of himself. During a year or more the work has
been re-read, corrected, weighed, taken up again, re-written.
When it finally appears, the author is in such a state of
anxious expectation that the smallest misprint is enough to

throw him into despair, and a forgotten word can torture him. Imagine when it is a chapter.

When an attentive friend telephoned to her what he had just observed, I saw Colette turn pale and I was worried. An annoyance or irritation of normal size would only have provoked her favourite: "In the name of thunder!" or some other such healthy explosion. Already she was telephoning to the publisher to point out to him that some copies of the book were coming out incomplete. It was soon discovered that the entire printing of 35,000 volumes, already distributed, was mutilated.

What had happened? Correcting proofs is a most detailed occupation which it is impossible to do all at one go. In resuming it after a more or less long interval, Colette had not checked the continuity of the chapters and the whole bundle of proofs was passed by her for press. The publisher was therefore relieved of responsibility. All the same I think he would have withdrawn the volumes from circulation, as Colette begged him to do, if this operation had still been possible. But all that could be done was to restore the text for the next printings, which in future comprised 278 pages instead of 246.

Colette remained gloomy about it for some time. It was not her vanity as an author which was concerned, for she really had none. It was her conscience, her love of work well done, her exactitude. She neglected nothing that concerned her job, even busying herself with the placing of the title and the other statements on the covers of her books. This book which the public might think had been tossed off in an off-hand way was the last thing which she could take lightly.

Did she work with as much difficulty as she has let it be thought, and was that constant felicity of expression only due to laborious research? If one studies her manuscripts one sees that the essential—the fresh image, the bold concision—is there in the first draft. It was the turn of her sentences which Colette worked over the most, as if she wanted to make them always more faithful to her own internal rhythm, in harmony with her exacting ear. The arrangement of her novels, their unfolding, gave her a great deal of trouble. She preferred beginning again to correcting and, being prudent, she proceeded by pages rather than by sections.

She was wise enough never to write in the morning, but to go out for a walk with her dog, whatever the weather, and for choice in the Bois de Boulogne. She never worked in the evening except when pressed by circumstance. It was chiefly between three and six in the afternoon that she composed that immense volume of work: fifty volumes, without counting the very numerous chronicles which have not yet been gathered together. If one considers, too, the theatrical adaptations, the dialogues for films, the lectures, a hundred different enterprises, the five or six letters which, never having known how to use a secretary, she wrote every day, full, spontaneous letters with never an erasure, and the dedications which she never refused, is one not tempted on the contrary to speak of exceptional facility, stripping that word of all disparaging implications?

Two suicides, that of Chéri and that of Michel in *Duo*—that is not too much in a romantic output, somewhat inclined to pessimism. Most of Colette's novels end with the defeat of love. Perhaps she always dreaded such a thing for herself, before she discovered that tenderness can be a delicious prolongation of love, that still preserves it complete.

To only one of her books, *Gigi,* did she give a really happy ending, and for that she has been reproached. The offer of marriage made to that little slip of a girl, the pupil of two former *demi-mondaines,* by the ultra-rich middle-class Gaston, struck people as unlikely. They said that it weakened this story which is so charged with penetrating observation and fierce humour. Cinderella and Prince Charming should be left for fairy stories!

But in so far as *Gigi* is a true story, as it very largely is, this end was imposed on Colette. Which is to say that in life there are endings which do not suit romantic writings. It must be admitted that marriage does seem rather a tame ending to any story which is at all dramatically tense. After that, there is absolutely nothing more to say. One can only have recourse to the word "End," or hurry to bring down the curtain. Colette knows this so well that, in *Gigi,* she does not even end her final sentence: *"Mamita," he said, "will you do me the honour, the favour, give me the infinite joy of bestowing on me the hand . . ."*

As with nearly all writers, each of the characters of Colette has several models. It therefore took time for these different types to fuse together and become the heroes of a novel. *Gigi* affords an example. The novel was written in 1942, the story was related in my presence round about 1926.

"La Treille Muscate" was still quite a new toy for us, and whenever we could escape from Paris, even for short holidays, we fled to Saint-Tropez. I think that it was during the winter, because I seem to remember that night fell early.

As we could not get to Saint-Tropez at a reasonable hour, we stopped at Valescure, a suburb of Saint-Raphaël. Colette knew a hotel there, kept by two ladies from Paris. It was an ancient villa of the 1880 type, narrow, tall and white, which looked more like a boarding-house than a hotel. The two ladies were sisters, and one had had a successful career at the Opera and had a Spanish name.

We were the only clients in the hotel and we stayed for a long time chatting with the two women, who were thrilled to talk to someone and to talk about Paris. We spoke chiefly of their niece, the Gigi who was not called Gigi, and who a few years before had married the Gaston who was not called Gaston, a marriage which had astonished the world and staggered the *demi-monde*. They told us how this Gigi had been brought up from her earliest youth with the idea of attracting and captivating Gaston. The strictest of rules had guided her education. All the tastes and preferences of Gaston were known and every day Gigi was taught her Gaston, as other children are taught their scales on the piano. It then happened that, one fine day, Gaston, rewarding such a long and praiseworthy plan, made the proposal expected of him, which was to set the young Gigi up for a certain time as his mistress.

*Horresco referens,* Gigi refused. The announcement caused as much scandal as if the world had begun to turn in the other direction. Fortunately it was only the *demi-monde* that was concerned. Actual committees of elderly dames met together to comment upon the incredible event, and to deplore the perversity of the younger generation.

"But what's the matter, Gilda, you aren't saying any-thing," said one of the dames, addressing another who was reputed to be sagacious. "What do you think about it, she's mad, isn't she?"

"What I think," answered Gilda, taking a long pull at her cigarette. "What I think is that she's a child who is very well advised."

Well advised or not, Gaston made his proposal of marriage.

Fifteen years later Colette wrote *Gigi,* a little novel whose fortune has been and still is great. Instead of 1918, Colette situated its action just before 1900, because it was at that moment that, married to Monsieur Willy, she knew the world of the *demi-mondaines,* then at the height of its vogue. Madame Alvarez and Aunt Alicia have not a single feature in common with our two hostesses of Valescure, except that they are sisters, but it was the name of one of them which put it into Colette's head to give a Spanish name to Gigi's grandmother. From that to "a creamy complexion," to "an ample bust," and to "hair lustrous with brilliantine" and "too white a powder" is only a step. For Aunt Alicia I have an idea there were several models, one of whom would be Liane de Pougy. No doubt also the fact that one of our ladies of Valescure belonged to the Opera, gave Colette the idea of putting Andrée, Gigi's mother, the one who had not succeeded in "the profession," in the Opéra-Comique. As for Gaston, he is the one who is most closely modelled on the real person he represents, even physically.

These metamorphoses, these transposings, take place for the most part in the subconscious: when the novel finally presents itself to its author with all its characters, its setting and its development, he has very often forgotten the incident or anecdote which gave it birth.

With Colette, the happenings of her life had no influence whatever on the tone of her books. I would say that she was too much of an artist for that, if the word had not been so debased. In the same way, if a musician is writing a Spanish symphony, no matter if he happens to be in a Nordic country, even shivering with cold, his score will be heavy with an overheated atmosphere and a violent sensuality. *Gigi,* a novel full of humour and irony, was written during the war at the time when, because of me, Colette was in the greatest torment. *La Fin de Chéri,* a hard, bitter book, without a smile, was composed at a time when she had reason to feel unreservedly happy. I have already spoken of *La Naissance du Jour.* . . . When she was in a low state physically, she did not allow herself to write.

# IX

Pictures of Colette in her last years, when she had attained a smiling serenity, have been so widespread that I
should like to be able to show her in all the vivacity of her
maturity. There was something almost prodigious in her
vital energy. She would want ten things at a time and all of
them at once, keeping her household on tenter-hooks. Even
a visitor would be seized upon, enrolled and hustled. Hardly
had he brought her the object she wanted than he was sent
off on another mission. Colette meanwhile would be chang-
ing the furniture round, driving in a nail, running to the
telephone, cleaning the ears of one of her animals, receiving
three people on different affairs, signing a contract without
looking at it, climbing on a ladder and running to the
kitchen. All this with loud cries, cursings, ripples of laughter
and most comic sallies. Her plumpness did not prevent her
from remaining very supple, and she always preferred sitting
on the ground to a chair. She went barefoot as often as possible, shoes with heels having always incommoded her. The
day she discovered sandals, she adopted them for good.

Can one be surprised that, when she sat down at her work-table, she gave a sigh, especially because she knew she would not leave it until the moment came to put the top back on her pen, and that she would not for a single moment relax her determination to do well and to do better?

For the period that we are now considering, one can find some sketches drawn from life in a book by Claude Chauvière: *Colette,* published by Firmin-Didot in 1931. Claude Chauvière was for three years the secretary of Colette, who never knew how to use a secretary. Claude proved to be very unsuited to this job; her object, which she did not disguise, was to write a book on Colette, to find herself at the fountain-head of the documents, to seize Colette in her daily life so as to paint the most living possible portrait of her. She was a young woman full of talent and ardour, but also of melancholy. When she ceased to be under the tonic influence of Colette she had a momentary tendency to mysticism, and died young of a secret physical disease and a hidden despair.

Her book is very well done. There may be other views on the documents and literary appreciations which it contains, and as a picture of Colette in the ordinary run of her every-day life, it is irreplaceable. Claude Chauvière has noted Colette's very phrases and gestures. They are better than sketches, they are tracings:

" 'I'm hungry!' cries Colette, just as she cried a moment ago 'I'm thirsty!'

"Over-flowing with life and activity she glows with physical joy, hugging to her strong heart every thing that quivers with life, in order to embrace it, crush it, draw the very marrow out of it. Then, with her hands stretched out, off she goes into the world to seize more things and taste them all.

"In the intervals, passive, idling, and greedy, she munches apples and disembowels chocolate éclairs.

" 'Pauline! I'm going to faint with hunger!'

"The kindly Pauline, with her yellow eyes, is doling out the animals' food and remains quite calm. So then Colette arranges the fire, criss-crosses the logs, puts on coal, pokes it, pushes back the ashes, wields the bellows and then lights some sticks of what she calls 'smell-good.' These flames and the smoke intoxicate her.

"But a guest enters, Souci jumps at his throat in a friendly way, and Colette encourages him: 'Bite him, Souci, eat him up, he's late!'

"And here she is comparing sapphires. She immediately guesses their origin, their price and the best use to make of them. The cat solemnly winds her way between the carafes and the fruit-dishes. Colette strokes the precious stones: she feels at home with them. Then she carves the leg of lamb: she is at home there too.

" 'Are you warm, Claude?'

"(To Pauline) 'Turn on the radiator; she's pale, she's cold. I tell you you're cold. Yes, I'm keeping this nice fat knuckle end. . . . Maurice, put the salad into the dressing; it's better that way. How would it be if we drank some of my marc? I made eighteen litres of it this year.'

" 'You distil your own?'

" 'Souci, *will* you go to sleep! And quicker than that! Pauline, I shall take her to the vet, to her doctor I mean, she's got worms. . . .'

"Colette: 'Look, here's a tray-cloth I was embroidering when we lived in the Rue Jacob. D'you see, Claude dear, it's linen embroidered in self-colour. Now Pauline, show her the orange one with the black pattern, contrasting tones you see. What do you think of it? And show her my specialty too: nightshirts made in a day, and trimmed with crochet. There they are "same as I said." '

"I try to put some questions.

"But some ladies who are called Moune, the Countess, Nathalie, Miche, come through on the telephone and, thanks to it, Colette proceeds from Ferenczi to Flammarion, from Luc-Albert Moreau to Léon-Paul Fargue, from *Candide* to *Vogue*.

"And then Colette wants to go to the cinema. And then Colette has an appointment with her dressmaker for a fitting, another with Gaston for a hair-setting; and then she wants to go and buy mangos at H——, coffee from C——. And she has not yet powdered her face. . . .

"She bounds into the bathroom and we hear noises of taps and glasses. She sprays the apartment and freshens up the flowers. . . . But Colette has mislaid an index-file: the index-file of the living. There are three indexes: that of the dead, the one of publishers and the one which has disappeared. We open and close drawers and bookcases.

"Diversion. The telephone continues its work of uniting and separating, and people come in and go out as though in a mill. . . ."

Of course, that is only one view of Colette, the rhythm of a life rather than that life itself, the mode and the time of a piece of music more than its melody. But how much more precious do such notations seem to me than many an article written with care. Let me take, for example, in this same book by Claude Chauvière, a "piece" signed by me, which Claude asked me to write on "La Gerbière," a property which Colette and I possessed for a year at Montfort-l'Amaury in 1930. My only reason for reproducing this piece of writing is to illustrate my point:

"In thrall successively to sweet but harsh Brittany, the antique land of the Limousin, and the flamboyant South, Colette only inhabited one house in the Ile de France. This was a little middle-class two-storey dwelling on the high promontory which dominates Montfort-l'Amaury, but looking away from the town. Its two principal façades, meeting at right angles, bounded a rose garden. In summer, ancient shrubs bent under the weight of flowers with forgotten names. But another part of the property advanced like a prow towards a vast landscape which, plunging suddenly into the valley, revealed in the distance a huge sky for ever in movement. Thus Colette's taste for restrained horizons, sheltered houses, dwellings cut to a normal man's measure, and also her need for large airy spaces, were both satisfied. But she will only admit a panorama if she can banish it at will, and she would not have tolerated this one if there had not been a hundred yards of lawn between herself and it. She likes to say: 'You must never allow a landscape to come into the house without your permission.'

"Garden, lawn, little wood descending abruptly towards the road, a diligent hand, while respecting your country-fied wilderness, peppered you with bulbs in winter, with layerings and new plantations, and tied artificial nests to the trunks of your trees. For even before there was a piece of furniture in the house, the birds were provided for and a profusion of nuts was offered to hypothetical squirrels. Anyone who has not seen Colette in the spring eagerly on the lookout for the births of hyacinths, lilies of the valley, young tits, slow-worms and the flowers of the whitebeam, all mixed together in the same pagan love, is ignorant of the profound sources from which she draws.

"In winter, not even the worst downpour prevented her from coming to the little house at Montfort. It is from Colette I learn that there is no true winter in our climates, but that a perpetual up-thrust towards life goes on under the humus. An old gardener with whom she used to exchange mysterious remarks knew this too. Unable either to read or write, isolated from the world like a blind person, his knowledge was never at a loss over things that are really important to know. Often Colette and he, their faces lit by the same conniving smile, would both indulge in strange graftings or prepare baleful drugs for I know not what purpose.

"For she adores heavy work and hard natural effort. Fire, that element so many of us find rebellious, obeys her marvellously, smouldering all night under the ashes which she piles up according to certain rites, reviving at her first word, springing up and lying down like any other household pet. And how many times, seeing that hand of hers, small and hard, grubbing, instead of using the garden rake which takes too long, scratching the soil and pulling up ivy roots, have I not felt full of wonder, as a child who imagines that the melody is born from the fingers of the pianist, that that same hand should hold the pen which honours poetry."

The first defect of this over-written article is that I talk about Colette in it rather than show her. It is impossible to live in an open-hearted way with someone and at the same time observe her gestures and note her words. Perhaps books about the great ought to be written only by their secretaries.

Yet Sido was more fortunate. Three pages of Colette and we know the whole of her. I shall never sufficiently marvel at it.

"La Gerbière" belonged to me, as "La Bergerie" had previously. It was mere chance that their names should have been anagrammatic. Those who see signs everywhere can meditate on that one. For my part I see nothing in it. I only know that I soon had to sell "La Gerbière," which was caught up in the tornado which blew upon the luxury trade during the American crisis and left me ruined. It was Mademoiselle Chanel who bought it.

# X

AFTER *La Naissance du Jour,* without drawing a breath, Colette wrote *La Seconde,* which appeared the year after, in 1929. In order to finish this novel she went, during a mild and rainy February, to "Le Château d'Ardenne," an hotel in the Belgian Ardennes, whose wooded slopes she hardly had a chance to appreciate, so furiously did she work. She considered *La Seconde* one of her best novels, although this small restricted drama, deliberately written in a low key, did not obtain the same following as her other works.

The periodicals fought for every novel of Colette's. In the case of *La Seconde* it was the friendly insistence of Pierre Brisson which won the day on behalf of *Les Annales,* which his mother, Yvonne Sarcey, edited. Colette took a lot of coaxing, for *Les Annales* was a family journal destined especially for young girls, who at that time still occasionally agreed to read what was meant for them.

"I know you, Pierre," said Colette, "you will ask me to make cuts."

Pierre Brisson swore that *Les Annales* was just then in process of transforming itself, and seeking a much wider audience, and ready, on that account, to accept the most daring things that could be written.

When he received the copy there were indeed a few embarrassed telephone calls: "Dear friend, I am going to ask you to water down something very slightly, which won't change the sense at all. . . ."

The first storm over, Colette put a little water into her wine, Pierre Brisson did the same until, from compromise to compromise, the book was judged fit to be left in many hands, if not all.

When Colette received the first number of *Les Annales* in which *La Seconde* was appearing, she calmly took up the receiver and called Pierre Brisson:

"Dear friend, was it worth while asking me what you call waterings-down, in order to add to my text obscenities of your own making?"

"What, dear friend?" answered a stupefied voice.

"Perhaps you will be kind enough to look for yourself, page so and so, line . . ."

At the other end of the telephone there was a dismayed silence, as Pierre Brisson read in *Les Annales* the following sentence: "*Jane coupa son fils d'un coup de dents.*" *

"I told you," said Colette mercilessly, "that it would end in cuts!"

Yesterday Paul Abram warned me that he had arranged for the voice of Colette to be heard on the radio, by using some old recordings taken from a record library. They were readings made by Colette at different times. The first was

---

* The misprint was *fils* (son) for *fil* (thread); viz., "Jane cut off her son with a snap of her teeth."

the farewell letter from *La Vagabonde*. Her voice is excellent and no one could read better, with simpler and truer intonation. Next the lines concerning Ravel taken from the chapter entitled "A Drawing-Room in 1900" in the *Journal à Rebours*. Finally, this portrait of Debussy which, after *Trait pour Trait*, figures in *En Pays Connu*, and shows the composer a prey, with the intensity of a crisis, to the effort of musical memory:

"We were together one Sunday evening when we had heard played, for the first time in France, *Antar*, unless perhaps it was *Schéhérazade*, and Debussy, obsessed and captivated, was singing the symphony inside himself as he remembered it. A sort of humming like that of a hive or a telephone pole came from him, a fumbling, undecided murmur. Then the memory came more sharply and his closed expression cleared suddenly.

" 'Wait! Wait!' he said very loud. 'Like this . . . mmmm . . . and like that: mmmm. . . .' One of us seized the melodic fragment which he had just found again and spun it out.

" 'Yes, yes!' cried Debussy, 'And in the meantime there are the cellos deep down saying: mmmm. . . . And the kettle-drums, Heavens above, the kettle-drums, merely a sort of quivering which announces the explosion of the brass, and . . . and . . .'

"With his mouth closed, and then whining as he imitated the violins, he panted, pulled in all directions by the resonances which were fighting in his memory; seizing the poker, he used it to beat on the rosewood case of the piano. With his free hand he went 'zzziii!,' all down the window-pane, then clapped his lips drily to recall the xylophone, and said 'doog, doog' in a crystalline voice to convey to us the liquid drops of the 'Mustel' organ. . . ."

Colette speaks this passage in an extraordinary way. She restores to us Debussy giving birth to the melody, growling, groaning, panting. She replaces the "mmmm's" by the actual air of *Antar* which Debussy was outlining. I don't think one could go further in the evocation of someone through a text, and the accent and movement of speech.

For my part I saw not only Debussy but also the woman who was reading. I confess that I had hesitated to listen in: can there be any crueller consolations than a film or a record? So much and so little!

Last year, in Brussels, in the course of an evening reception given in honour of Colette, I had not been able to avoid looking at the film on her life which was made in our house. Sitting in the royal box I had at all costs to control myself. I had less difficulty in doing this, in spite of the scenes which show Colette and myself talking together, than when I found myself alone to-day with a voice!

There was the adventure of the beauty products. It surprised most people and occasioned commentaries which were not all kind. What was this new extravagance? A second profession? Was not Colette earning enough money with her own work? When one held the place that she occupied in the world of letters, one did not "lower oneself" from love of money, by undertaking a trade which at that time had a slightly unsavoury reputation. Or else was her aim merely to get herself talked about, to astonish once again, even by means of shoddy publicity?

Colette's motives were always much more simple. Her

work and the hours of concentrated immobility which she imposed on herself every day, when the movement of life was calling to her so strongly, had ended by creating in her a furious desire to escape from the constraint. After *La Naissance du Jour* in 1928 she had produced, in 1929 alone, *La Seconde, Sido,* and two other short texts, *Renée Vivien* and *Regarde.* "I've got nothing more to say," she maintained.

In addition she was feeling the need to renew contact with unknown people, with those ordinary folk who have always been her true characters, because it is only with them that a drama takes on its universal meaning. For too long now she had been living away from the people she used to meet in the music-hall, on tour, and later in her office at *Le Matin.* She wanted to do a real job, a human job, which would let her come and go, travel, handle objects and knead substances.

The idea of fabricating and selling beauty products had been put into her head by André Maginot, the man after whom the Maginot Line was named.

"Already at that time I had the idea of fabricating perfumes and some beauty products. I confess that my commercial zeal met with no encouragement.

"For my friends and myself I used to boil the flesh of quinces and the mucilaginous envelope of their seeds. I beat the cold cream and pressed out the juice of cucumbers. . . . Why not? The Duchess Sforza, born Antokolski, set me an example when she fitted up an ancient apothecary shop.

"The first time, after his serious war-wound, that André Maginot came, walking painfully, to lunch with us again in the Boulevard Suchet, I installed him in the biggest armchair and slipped a low bench under his injured leg. He made fun of me to hide the fact that he was accepting these attentions with embarrassment. The garden, small but well-planted, the cat and the tortoise were the subject of conversation while we were alone. Then Maginot asked me suddenly if I was still thinking of my 'luxury trade.' 'Not often,' I said truthfully.

" 'You are wrong, this is the moment to think about it. I am speaking seriously. A strange period is about to begin. Those who try something new will only risk making a mistake. And if they do they only have to start again. The important thing is to try. And the pleasant side of it will be to escape, by means of one activity, from another activity, not to let yourself be cornered. . . . In your case I would go bald-headed for it. I see so clearly how it ought to be launched. On the door of the shop I should write . . .'

"He threw his arms apart. His right hand reached as far as a Moustier plate on the wall, which tinkled, his left arm disappeared through the French window, casting its shadow on the gravel:

" 'I should write: "I am called Colette and I sell scents." ' "

Colette told me of her plan and asked me to realise it for her. I did my best to dissuade her, but the arguments which would have weighed with anyone else were powerless with her. I showed her that her fame might risk being tarnished by it, but the word fame was a dead letter for her, and she asked me why all trades people were not put in prison, if I thought it dishonourable to indulge in trade.

I pointed out to her that the manipulation of the quinces, cucumbers and other heady substances would only take a certain time and that to compete with the other firms of beauty products she would have to imitate them in the way their managers gave frequent demonstrations, in which they treated and made up their clients themselves. This idea put the finishing touch to her temptation. She always adored busying herself with the human face, she used to change the hair style of her friends, using the scissors for it, and even an unknown visitor would not be spared. Already she saw herself modifying women's faces, restoring their true characters to them, manipulating colours, plunging her hands deep into pastes and unguents!

There remained for me only one means of preventing this enterprise and that was to refuse her my help. The decision was a serious one. There was no doubt I saw much better than Colette the difficulty of establishing and exploiting such a business in the midst of a commercial crisis. But if she succeeded, once the initial period was over, I was sure that Colette would return to her writer's bench with merely a little less uncertainty for the morrow. Then again, a failure, after a few days of disappointment, would be quickly forgotten. But on the other hand if I made her give up the idea and she felt herself once again inescapably cornered, she would never cease to regret it. Knowing her as I did, she would be consoled for having failed, but not for not having undertaken.

This was not the only time when I chose to let her steer her way among the rocks, ready to right the helm when shipwreck threatened rather than put obstacles in her way.

In the early days the business gave Colette all that she expected of it. Nothing was more amusing than the visits to the laboratories which manufactured our products, nothing more beautiful than the test-tubes and retorts. It was a question of choosing, testing, tasting, sniffing. She busied herself with the bottles, the boxes and the packaging. All the prospectuses and the instructions on usage were written by her, and for the cover of the powder boxes she drew her own caricature. I have kept nothing of all that but I hope some amateurs have taken it on themselves to do so.

A pretty shop in the Rue de Miromesnil bore the name of Colette. The opening day had all the appearance of a Parisian event. For a year Colette went there regularly, making up her clients herself and traveling into the provinces too, to give long demonstrations there, like a good and conscientious businesswoman. People crowded there; but at the end of her treatment the client would bring out of her bag one or two books to be autographed, proving that you cannot get rid of literature so easily. What was more, Colette's dream of ceasing to write was not realised; she was working as much as ever. It is possible not to like a thing and yet to have the habit of it, to cling to your enemies as much as your friends.

The products were good, the business acquired a small clientele. To develop it, even to keep it going, new capital was necessary. Before begging for this we had to take our bearings. It was now clear that the business would still need the personal work of Colette for several years. The absurdity of this began to be evident even to her eyes. The illusion that she could rest from writing was dispelled. The demonstrations in the provinces were often followed by literary lectures, which caused a twofold fatigue, of which Colette tried to say nothing. But she had to admit that her efforts were more usefully employed in her real profession. The time had come to recognise her mistake and turn the page as quickly as possible.

What did the balance-sheet of the venture show? Apparently a great waste of time. However, nothing is less certain. The enterprise had helped Colette to overcome a moment of distaste for her job as a writer, and at the same time had put her in touch with a numerous public which would give her a chance to find fresh themes. Before long now she was to begin the series of her short novels which are so human and so stark. For instance it may be that the truth of a character like "the wife of the photographer" owes everything to the time that Colette spent among ordinary mortals.

Just before she took up the beauty-products business, Colette had brought out, in 1932, *Ces Plaisirs*. . . . It is the most difficult of her books and the most original. I doubt whether anything so penetrating has been written on the senses, and particularly the sexual senses, on their sovereignty and their sadness. Some people rate it very high, but it is a book that disconcerted most readers. It had begun to appear in the weekly *Gringoire* but the director stopped publication after the second instalment, in a letter to Colette that ran somewhat like this: "Dear friend, this time it is too much. I am receiving protests from all sides and so I'm forced . . ."

It is true that ten years earlier, although less brutally, *Le Blé en Herbe* had suffered the same fate. The novel was appearing on the story-page of the newspaper *Le Matin*, headed "The Thousand and One Mornings." Each chapter formed a separate story, had to be of a fixed length and to have a title. It is astonishing that such conditions did not upset the harmonious progress of the book. A little more than half-way through, the directors of *Le Matin* stopped publication of *Le Blé en Herbe*. So much freedom allied to such modesty of expression, such a penetrating analysis of feminine motives, such simplicity, had been "too much" for many readers of *Le Matin*.

The work benefited by this. If you glance through it, keeping this in mind, you notice this cutting up into short lengths, right up to the chapter beginning "We finish here, this year . . ." which in one long flowing passage gathers together and unravels the main threads of the drama. The effect of it is great, and one might attribute it to an outstanding skill in composition if one did not know that this arrangement is merely the result of an independence recovered by chance.

If *Ces Plaisirs* had been written in a didactic strain no doubt it would have been praised to the skies; it would have been said that the problem of the senses had been treated for the first time in a true philosophical spirit, that . . . But the book is written with Colette's habitual limpidity, all in short recitals, more or less disguised memories, and anecdotes. It tackles the question of sexual anomalies with assurance, leaving nothing in obscurity. Although, so it is said, only a scientific vocabulary or heavy irony suits such questions, Colette devoted to them the same sharpness of observation and the same respect as she gave to other vital manifestations. With her classic tendency towards unity, she claimed that there is only one love, that everywhere its language and its movement are the same, both among those who, as in *Le Blé en Herbe,* are discovering it, or in those who can accept as partners only others who resemble themselves.

The fact that the book leads in the end to bitter conclusions is not the fault of Colette, but that of "those pleasures. . . ." A single work such as that would be enough to bring a writer glory. In the output of Colette, whose richness becomes every day more apparent, it is only one book more which some time or other will be judged at its true worth.

Colette borrowed the title from herself, after the manuscript had been called for a certain time *Le Fourbe*. It is the beginning of a sentence from *La Naissance du Jour:* "those pleasures which are lightly called physical." I proposed another to her: *Le Pur et l'Impur,* which she preferred, but the publisher insisted on keeping the first. Colette always regretted it and seized the opportunity of a new and slightly augmented edition, in 1943, to impose her choice at last. She explained why in a very brief preface destined for her collected edition:

"It is according to my own wish that the volume entitled *Ces Plaisirs* . . . shall in the future be called *Le Pur et l'Impur.*

"If I had to justify such a change I could only do so on the grounds of a strong liking for crystalline sounds, and a certain dislike for incomplete titles ending in dots—neither of them very important reasons after all."

# XI

I NEVER KNEW HER to sleep very well. Later on pain gave her many sleepless nights, but on waking she was always in good spirits, alert, and as if facing life anew. Except in the country, where Colette got up before anyone else, Pauline would come in to draw her curtains and at once there was a torrent of questions and demands: "What's the weather like? Pauline, what does the thermometer show? What does the barometer say? Give me my watch! Where is my powder? Bring me my work, I must tear up what I did last night, it's no good. Have you been out? Who did you see? What are we going to eat to-day? Where are the newspapers? Just look at the shape of that cloud! Give me the case of butterflies on the left up there, I must look at something!"

I would come into her room, but never before she'd been tidied and adorned, with her face made up. She discovered me and greeted me every morning, as she discovered the rest of the world. She talked to me of the book which she had gone on reading long after I had gone to bed, and which most often was a travel book. The travels she preferred were those of the mid-nineteenth century, because of the imagination and innocence of their authors. They still left for redoubtable and unknown parts of Africa in straw hats and button boots, accompanied by their dogs which inevitably perished there. Colette would tell me of a meeting with a Negro king, or a hunt full of adventures, as if she had actually taken part in it. Or else it would be a dream which had remained in her mind in all its vividness.

Pauline brought in breakfast with the newspapers and the post. Colette split open her croissant with a knife without ever letting a crumb fall, and goodness knows how difficult that is, buttered it slowly and salted the butter. She took very little milk and a lot of sugar in her coffee, and—yes indeed!—she dipped her croissant in it just as does every French person and no English person who respects himself.

Once upon a time I should not have related these insignificant details of daily life. I am modelling myself here on Colette's interviewers, particularly the foreigners. "Do you drink coffee in the morning, or tea?" But perhaps these questions are not merely the fruit of what I will be bold enough to call "starism," and there really is in every author a tea-behaviour or a coffee-behaviour. Who knows if the fact that Colette salted her butter did not tinge her whole day with a country colour and have an influence on her work?

I have just been looking at Bernard Gavoty's program "The Great Interpreters" on television, which showed Igor Markevitch, the conductor. The program ended with a fragment of the *Symphonie Fantastique* of Berlioz, directed by Markevitch, after Gavoty had declared: "I don't like, I've never been able to like that symphony," to which Markevitch had replied: "For my part I like it very much and I'll try, in conducting it, to make you share my liking for it."

Colette had a great weakness for the *Symphonie Fantastique,* which she knew by heart and never tired of hearing. Is it not remarkable that in her musical and literary preferences she proved herself so romantic, whereas there was little of this in her way of living and in her work?

Her ear and her memory for music were faultless and she was never mistaken as to either the key or the tone of what she was hearing, being particularly sensitive to the exactness of the movements, and able to read a score. She did not greatly value the old composers, with the exception of Bach, whom she called "a sublime sewing-machine." Mozart left her cold. On the other hand she could herself have conducted the symphonies of Beethoven or *La Damnation de Faust* and she loved the German romantics. The infatuation which she had had for Wagner, in the time of Monsieur Willy and his friends, had cooled off. Brahms did not touch her in any way. But Fauré, Debussy and Ravel. *L'Enfant et les Sortilèges* drew tears from her.

One day she summoned to the side of her divan-raft the great conductor Münch to have a talk with him about the movements of the *Symphonie Fantastique.* He accepted the invitation with a good grace, and can hardly have forgotten the ardour which she put into it.

She wrote words for music by Poulenc, by Jean-Michel Demase when he was still a child, and even by Reynaldo Hahn, who failed to feel inspired and sent her back her little poem many years later, when he was already on the point of death, with this disillusioned little note:

Dear friend,

I have found again this charming little thing which I was not able to use. Blame nothing but my decrepitude.

I return it to you because another musician would perhaps be very happy if you entrusted him with it, and I don't want it to get lost in the chaos of paper which envelopes and submerges me.

We never see each other any more. It's very sad. Everything is very sad!

Your faithful admirer.

Here is the little poem:

### THE PEARL

Toad with the beautiful eyes,
Have you found my pearl
That I lost last night?
It hung from a golden thread
Between my two breasts.

I was here in this alley,
Alone, and I thought to myself
That my pearl was round as the moon
And as white, touched, too,
With rose, like my breasts.

Toad with the beautiful eyes,
I stayed alone there in the alley,
Nor strayed save when for an instant,
I leant from the boundary wall
To say "Good evening, my neighbour!"

"Young girl who knows how to lie,
Yes, I have found your pearl.

It lay where the grass is still warm,
In the place that you have not named.
There, young girl, did I drink,

With the other pearls that you left,
Of the dew and the tears of your joy
The pearl that you lost in the grass.
Hear its sound in my crystal throat:
        Oo . . . Oo . . . Oo . . ."

And Colette indicates that "Oo . . . Oo . . . Oo . . ." should
imitate the call of the toad.

In addition to *L'Enfant et les Sortilèges* by Ravel, for
which Colette wrote the libretto, Albert Wolff set to music
a fairy ballet by her, *The Beheaded,* which has not up to the
present been performed.


*Ces Plaisirs* in 1932, *La Chatte* in 1933, *Duo* in 1934, and
besides these some lesser works—the selling of beauty-products had in no way slowed down Colette's production. And
I have made no mention of her numerous contributions to
the press, her dramatic criticisms in *Gringoire* and in *La
Revue de Paris,* and her lectures. In her spare moments she
changed living quarters.

Definitely ruined—I was going to say ruined at last—I gave
up business, which had always bored me, to devote myself
to journalism, the dream of my life. Thenceforward Colette
and I had identical occupations and the same hours of
work and leisure. Our paradoxical understanding, made up
of so many differences and profound agreement on the essentials, was more than ever strengthened by this. Right up
to the moment when she breathed her last, we never left

each other of our own accord, except for a few hours every day, meeting always with undiminished pleasure. We made this long journey hand in hand and that is not a mere figure of speech.

That is why this essay could hardly be written as an ordinary biography. Nothing would happen in it. Happiness has no adventures. How much more there was to tell in the existence of Madame de Staël, when Benjamin Constant dragged her by her hair from the top to the bottom of the staircase at the Château de Coppet!

What! Never a betrayal? No, and not even one of those groundless scenes which are daily bread in many households. Chance would have it that neither of us liked such things. But every moment that we lived together was a moment of fullness and silent joy. I have nothing more romantic to offer.

Colette has spoken in *Trois . . . Six . . . Neuf* of her moving about, pretending that she was not specially fond of this and attributing it to fate. The truth is that she was both stay-at-home and adventurous, and how can one better combine these contradictory tendencies than by moving house?

At one time she had had a gipsy for a nurse, and she made her responsible for her liking for moving house, when she would admit it. A gipsy, and not a man, as it may be supposed if one day a dedication which she gave during the war is found again. The man in question used to let her have the whitest possible milk at the price of the blackest possible market. Being sentimental into the bargain, he asked for "a little word on a book." Colette wrote: "To Monsieur X, who nourished me with his milk." This inscription makes a pendant to another, a reward for services at least as illicit: "To my black angel."

Moving days began with a burst of war-music and gave rise to an orgy of manual tasks. It was all that Colette and Pauline could do not to transport the furniture on their own backs. At five in the evening the new apartment looked like a workshop with stacks of baskets, pieces of furniture limping from the strain of the migration and straw clinging obstinately to every corner. A persistent draught raised dust which made man and beast sneeze. Even so does the wind sweep across the battlefield on the evening of a disaster.

This was the moment that Colette would choose, with an innocent air, to entrust me with long and complicated errands. When I returned three hours later, I would find a warm, gay apartment where the things looked as though they had been settled in their final places for years. Pictures and engravings were hung, a wood fire was crackling in the hearth with the animals dozing in front of it. Colette would enjoy my amazement: "I've performed another miracle," she would say, heaving a sigh in which weariness warred with contentment.

At the end of 1934 we left the Hotel Claridge, but not the Champs-Elysées, to go and perch on the top story of the Marignan building, on the side giving on to the Rue de Marignan. It was an immense new construction with thin walls and partitions that echoed like the nave of a church. A sneeze on the first floor shook the windows on the sixth floor. What had attracted Colette to this apartment, which was rented by the yard like a piece of cloth, was a big balcony which formed a terrace where she proposed to make flowers climb, and especially to cultivate strawberries in pots. During the three years that we passed in this market-place I can certify that the crop never exceeded three or four strawberries a season.

At Claridge's we occupied neighbouring rooms, but we had not yet shared a house in common and it was expedient to safeguard the proprieties. We took great trouble to this end, getting them to put in separate entrances and bells, pro-tecting partitions and separate telephones, all of which cost a considerable amount. After which it occurred to us that it would perhaps have been simpler to marry.

Once the idea was put forward it seemed to us both prac-tical and attractive. We were very sure, after ten years, how much we enjoyed living together. Friendship contributes more to this than love, and the friendship which accompanies love has a rare and incomparable flavour. A signature in a *mairie* would in no way change our reciprocal feelings, ex-cept by adding to them an act of trust and kindness, a re-spectability in our relations which seemed to us touching, an increased impression that we were pulling the same wagon. However banal they may be, the terms "my wife" and "my husband" become words of tenderness when that tenderness exists.

For such a simple formality there was no point in rousing the masses and still less the reporters and photographers. When I asked to be excused from publishing the banns, the official at the *Préfecture* whom I approached said to me: "Your desire for discretion is not a sufficient reason. The only motive that you could put forward is the fear of scan-dal. So just tell me that, since your district has thought you were married for a long time, it would create a scandal if they were to learn, precisely through your marriage, that you were not. Then I can give you the necessary permission." I hastened to combine our wish to be left in peace and our care for public morality.

We were married on April 3, 1935, at eleven in the morning at the *Mairie* of the 8th *Arrondissement,* which had witnessed my birth forty-five years before. It hardly lasted more than ten minutes, after which we took our witnesses to lunch in the country at Vaux-de-Cernay, in an inn called "Au Père Léopold," whose country cooking we liked. The menu, which we had ordered, consisted of an omelette à la crème, and little plump, smooth knuckles of ham. We had to imagine the absent violinists, fiddling at a village festivity.

On our way home, between two sunny intervals, snow began to fall, snow with large flakes of dazzling whiteness. Colette asked me to stop the car and got down to receive this impalpable manna rapturously on her face. She never remembered the date of April 3, being generally forgetful of anniversaries, but she always remembered that springtime snow, to the point of speaking of it eleven years later in *L'Etoile Vesper.*

# XII

VIRTUE IS ALWAYS rewarded, but rarely as quickly as in the case with which we are concerned. We were invited for the first crossing, the "maiden voyage" of the *Normandie,* arranged for June 4th, 1935. If we had not been married, our living together in prim New York would have presented not inconsiderable problems for us.

Accustomed though they are to spectacles proclaimed long in advance with a flourish of trumpets, young people to-day can have little idea of the clamour that was made about this voyage. For months the newspapers had described in detail this 80,000-ton liner, the biggest which had ever been built, the fastest and most luxurious. The result of collaboration between all our industries, it would carry beyond the seas the prestige of French quality, as yet uncontested.

One fine morning Colette, who was reporting for *Le Journal,* and I took the special train for Le Havre, which had been put at our disposal. The newspapers had spread themselves about the abundance which we should find on board. The fare would be unrivalled and among the tons of victuals on board caviare would appear as the commonest of hors d'oeuvres.

Nevertheless, Colette turned up at the outset with a basket full of provisions on her arm: home-made pâté, hard-boiled eggs and a cold chicken made it clear that country wisdom scorns contingencies. The rumour of this spread through the train. The journalists, gloating, made it their first news item. But as the hour was very early, and in the hurry of departure more than one breakfast had been neglected, the visits of our colleagues became more and more frequent and more and more interested, so that the basket was emptied long before we reached Le Havre.

The *Normandie* certainly looked very imposing and most elegant in its lines, and as soon as one was inside her, she gave a very good idea of a palace which had been set adrift, thanks to a new flood. About three thousand Parisian notables, a public half first-night and half charity-show, were to lead a life of gossip, carefully secluded from the sea, for four and a half days.

The liner had taken so long to build that its sumptuous decoration was already becoming old-fashioned. The stern, at the speed at which we were travelling, vibrated so much that it was necessary to evacuate part of it. In the state-room which preceded the great, cathedral-like dining-room, a colossal and glaringly gilded statue representing France, Paris or some allegory of that kind, shuddered violently. "The statue of terror," said Colette as she passed in front of it.

Once our initial curiosity was satisfied, the crossing became rather monotonous. Colette and Claude Farrère relieved this by exchanging the detective stories which they had brought with them.

The mastodon in the meanwhile clove its way through the sea in the hope of gaining the Blue Ribbon. The radio on board was at that time only a fragile link with the Continent. The journalists besieged it, and the Minister of Commerce, who was on board as representative of the government, doubtless had no access to it, since he kept on asking us: "Do you happen to know if I am still Minister?" Five days without a crisis seemed difficult for him to envisage. It must be admitted that the government—I can't remember now which it was—was on its last legs when he left.

New York was approaching. That approach, and the first skyscrapers emerging from the morning mist, have often been described, as has the arrival of the *Normandie,* which surpassed all our expectations. The whole city was gathered on the quayside, every boat that could sail came to meet us, and all the sirens blared.

The press, which had long since come on board, was already taking part in a real rat-hunt, with the aim of running to earth the personalities whose names had been mentioned to them.

Although nowadays Colette's name is familiar to the great public through the films, the theatrical presentations of *Gigi* and the popular editions, at that time she was only known in the United States to a few people. So she would easily have got out of all this if one of the reporters had not suddenly noticed, round-eyed, her bare feet in sandals, the toenails painted carmine. It was an unhoped-for chance. That she was a writer into the bargain did not add to the attraction, it was only a pity that she did not write with her feet. There was a rush. A clever mass movement cut Colette off from all retreat and the flashbulbs popped, followed by a running fire of questions:

"Why have you got bare feet?"

"Because it's comfortable for walking," was the answer which figured in the newspapers next day, like a riddle.

"How long do you take to write a novel?"

"Not long enough!"

"Have you written a novel during the crossing?"

"No, but you make me think I ought to have."

This dialogue of the deaf having ended, we were able to go up to the bridge to enjoy the spectacle.

Our first contact with American organisation and efficiency was disappointing. Never had so great a number of travellers arrived at the same time in the customs house, where there soon reigned a disorder surpassing all imagination, even ours. After we had waited standing for some hours, Colette was exhausted, so I took her away, trusting to luck that we should get our luggage. This was exactly what we ought to have done.

Half an hour later, from the 24th story of the Hotel Waldorf-Astoria, we were watching New York light her thousands of windows. Colette's French moderation was at no time shocked by the enormity of American architecture, whose beauty she at once recognised. "One's astonishment only lasts a moment," she said to me. "As soon as one's eye gets accustomed, it's only a question of proportions, and I like these."

We had to return two and a half days later with the *Normandie,* which did not leave us much time to inspect a new continent. So we made two important decisions. The first was to avoid all the more or less official ceremonies and

A FAMILY GROUP: 1891

Colette, about 1910

*Right:* "La Treille Muscate."
Etching by Dunoyer de Sogonzac. 1932

Honeymoon in New York. April 1935

The garden of the Palais Roy.

*Right:* At work under the "blue lantern"

THE REFLECTION OF COLETTE AMONG HER COLORED CRYSTALS

*Top right:* THE AUTHOR AND HIS WIFE

*Bottom right:* "OH, THAT CAT!"

COLETTE AT THE TIME OF HER 80TH BIRTHDAY, JANUARY 28TH, 1953

gatherings, beginning with a banquet for eight hundred people on the very night of our arrival. The second was to indulge in all our most private nonsense. Reminding ourselves that we were on our honeymoon, we decided to visit New York as would a young couple from Detroit or Pittsburgh.

We visited the top of the Empire State Building, where of course we had ourselves photographed in a becoming position, the "Roxy" with its six thousand seats, Central Park, and Harlem.

But even this program was seriously upset by Colette's discovery of Woolworth's, a chain of single-price stores such as did not yet exist in France. For five or ten cents they offered the customers thousands and thousands of articles, most of which appeared to me to be strictly unusable, but the sight of which produced in Colette a real intoxication. We spent hours in those frivolous places.

Another afternoon out of the two at our disposal was devoted to a pilgrimage: at the cost of a very expensive taxi-ride, we visited the head office of Parker Pens, Colette's favourites.

"But you can get the same in Paris," I said to her.

"They cost much less here, and besides they're fresher."

"That isn't very reasonable. A whole immense unknown world lies before us and we waste our time in shops. And what shops!"

"But what d'you want to visit then?" she said at last.

"The ramparts . . ." I answered emphatically.

I cannot remember anything else worth relating except our meeting with a cat on the evening when we were coming back from the "Roxy," our eyes still full of Mae West's hip-swinging. I had just said to Colette: "Conjure up a cat for us," when, conjured up or not, there was the cat, with its tail in the air, running towards Colette as if it had found a relation, and mewing.

"At last someone who speaks French," cried Colette.

She sat down, as was right and proper, on the edge of the pavement and the conversation began.

Our return from New York, in cabins chock-full of Woolwortheries, was accomplished without incident.

If a couple were forced to reveal everything about themselves, they would be more reluctant to betray their playful hours than their hours of passion. I have realised this in these notes on New York, when I have felt, in confessing our childishness, as if it were something immodest, because there is no greater abandon.

"Friends of ours sometimes exclaim with astonishment as soon as they come in: 'We heard you laughing, what had you got to make you laugh?' Sometimes we could have answered: 'He had me and I had him.'"

This was one of the last things which Colette wrote. She could have said nothing more significant about us.

This morning I received a bookseller's catalogue offering for sale twenty letters from Colette to "a well-known writer." I suspected, from certain quotations, that this must be Lucie Delarue-Mardrus. I hurried to the bookshop and it was indeed she. The letters were beautiful and I bought them. Through her adventurous life and a variety of gifts which led her from poetry to the novel, Lucie Delarue-Mardrus attained celebrity before Colette, so that Colette addressed her with a certain deference. In the same way, in the nineteenth century, one comes across very humble dedications from Flaubert and Baudelaire to Alexandre Dumas, as to an undisputed master: it is left to posterity to transpose the labels.

Later on they got on more familiar terms, but Lucie Delarue-Mardrus continued to keep Colette under her protecting wing. She examined her writings with care. When she did not understand a word which Colette had used, she declared that the word did not exist, or else that it stank of pedantry. But, as I have already said, these so-called "difficult" words were for Colette current terms which she often acquired in her childhood. Here is a letter which confirms it:

"But, darling, rest-harrow, we already called it by its name when I was a child in my village. Rest-harrow, or cammock. It's not my fault.

"As for the sense of smell . . . mine is so keen that it surpasses all the other senses. If my other senses were as good as my sense of smell I should be the queen of the world, or a hunting dog.

"I enjoy your accusing me and I enjoy defending myself against you. . . ."

There's the same reproach from Lucie Delarue-Mardrus, whose vocabulary was decidedly lacking in richness, about the words "barnacle" and "prasin." And the same kind of answer:

"Barnacle? My dear creature, if you had seen barnacles you'd know that you can't compare a barnacle . . . except with a barnacle. In any case they're quite common and they frequent our shores, O daughter of the sea! I love your remonstrating with me and I want no other 'schoolmistress'

than you. Come now, you're on familiar terms with 'chryso-
prase' and yet you cavil at 'prasin,' that word that applies
so precisely to the gilded green of cats' eyes? I am at your
disposal for all my 'chippings' as long as you wrap up your
reproaches in those poems which you so richly lavish on me,
scattering their leaves so generously. Who would not be
scolded at this price?"

All the same, it did sometimes happen, though very rarely,
that Colette hesitated over the sense of a word, but never
over its spelling. At such times everybody had to rush to
find dictionaries and works on botany and zoology. "Quick!
Quick!" she would cry. She never had a dictionary at hand
and would go for months without consulting one. She
seemed to possess words innately, and the use she made of
them was always as close to their Latin origin as possible. I
remember Monsieur Léon Bérard trying to make her admit
that she understood Latin and refusing to believe in her
denials. In a letter to Lucie Delarue-Mardrus Colette ex-
plains this once again: "Latin . . . How many times in my
life have I looked at it 'from outside,' with longing eyes.
It's too lofty for me."

But above all she used the exact name of objects in daily
use, which nowadays surprises people. Very often her poetry
arises less from the cloudy contour of a phrase than, on the
contrary, from the very precision of its terms and their
homely technicality. What in appearance could be less poetic
than a cheese? And yet:

"Not far away from my village *soumaintrains* were made,
and the red *saint-florentins* came to our market wrapped in
beetroot leaves. I remember that the long elegant leaves of

the sweet chestnut, with their serrated edges, were reserved
for the butter.

"To feel the crust, measure the elasticity of the texture,
and size up a cheese. . . . To study how a *camembert,* a *reblo-
chon* and a *marolles* crack their crusts, how the centre of a
*pont-l'évêque* forms a cushion or a hollow, to judge whether
a *munster* is distilling too liquid drops which threaten a
premature pungency, biting rather than smooth, are arts
which are gradually being lost."

There were so many arts which she had not lost. With her
the art of living came before the art of writing. She knew
a recipe for everything, whether it was for furniture-polish,
vinegar, orange-wine, quince-water, for cooking truffles or
preserving linen and materials. Pickling and steeping held
no mystery for her and everything smelt good and healthy.
This country wisdom impregnates all her work just as her
cupboards were always delicately fragrant. Looked at in one
light it would not even have displeased her if one talked of
recipes for writing.

Her opportunities for meeting Paul Valéry were infre-
quent, but when they met they were in close agreement.
Leaning towards each other they would whisper at great
length with an absorbed air. According to what Colette told
me, it was not of literature that they were speaking, but of
their craft and its alchemy, its taboos. So different in origin
and inspiration, these two superior craftsmen were in agreement over the secrets of workmanship, the tricks of the trade,
and golden numbers.

André Gide and she, on the other hand, though curious
about each other, when at last they found themselves together, had nothing to say to each other, and Gide ad-

mitted it. At long intervals, and most often without apparent motive, he wrote Colette a letter in which he would let himself go a little, then draw back, praise, and then criticise to give more weight to his praise, take one step forward and two backward. Colette had read little of Gide, but she liked his *Journals* in which she found something to feed on.

Very shortly before the death of Gide, Pauline came into my study one afternoon; I was there with a journalist friend.

"There is a gentleman downstairs in a car who has sent his daughter to know if Madame can receive him."

"Did he give his name?"

"Yes, it's something like Chide . . . Gide. Does Monsieur know it?"

I saw the journalist's eyes open wide. "Gide at Colette's," what an article! At my request he did not even make a mention of it, like a good friend and, that day at any rate, a bad journalist.

As soon as Gide was introduced, embarrassment was immediately evident. Colette, as during all her last years, was sitting on her divan-bed alongside her window that overlooked the Palais Royal. She was cordial, paid him great attention, called Gide "my pet" and talked to him of the Palais Royal, of gardens and birds. Gide remained strained and obviously out of his element. What did he expect Colette would talk to him about? Awkward and smooth all over, his extremely inquisitive eyes seemed to see nothing of the small enchanted world formed by the objects that surrounded Colette. He tried to throw a bridge between herself and him by speaking of his dog, which was eating the books. I observed with feeble comic humour that in effect there are several ways of enjoying books, I who have them bound and his dog who ate them. Colette seized on this talk about dogs, but was not followed. All that remained as a last resource was their health and their illnesses. The silences grew longer and longer until Gide rose. It was his first and last visit to Colette, a vain and touching attempt to adapt his angles to her roundness.

# XIII

JOURNALISM ENGROSSED HER more and more. In 1934 she agreed to write the weekly theatre column of the newspaper *Le Journal*. Theatre criticism had at that time a brilliance which it has lost. The two articles which carried weight were those of *Le Temps,* for which Pierre Brisson, after his father Adolphe Brisson, was responsible, and that of *Le Journal,* where Gide Pavlowski had succeeded Catulle Mendès. The fate of a play, the immediate future of an actor, depended in part on the verdicts pronounced from these lofty tribunes.

Colette installed herself, as always without assurance, behind this intimidating desk. At every first night, for five consecutive years, whenever one turned towards her box one could see her fluffy hair and pointed chin behind the lenses of her black opera-glasses, held by her short but delicate hand. Arriving before anyone else, she followed the show, motionless and deeply attentive.

Her article appeared on Sundays, and from then on the Sunday circulation of *Le Journal* increased. It was considered that Colette had discovered a new tone in criticism.

What in fact was new about her was that she did not change, that she did not possess two ways of observing or writing. "Impressionistic criticism" they called it, to which she would have replied "If you like," in so far as impressionism refuses to assign an order of merit between different styles, or to judge according to the rules.

With four or five evenings a week devoted to the theatre, and a long article to write which would not wait, it was hardly surprising if Colette's output of novels slowed down. Some people at that time deplored it. Only now is it beginning to be realised that these chronicles, collected each year under the title *La Jumelle Noire,* are of major importance in the work of Colette. As far as I know it was Thierry Maulnier who first underlined this in his *Introduction à Colette:*

". . . Their knowledge (of the four volumes of *La Jumelle Noire*) is, however, indispensable for anyone who wants to have an idea of the whole of the work of which they form, not an annex, a subsidiary part, but one of the most significant parts. First because of the literary perfection of each of these brief essays which, by virtue of the fact that they were originally destined for that most ephemeral of all forms of printed matter, the newspaper might well have seemed doomed to almost instantaneous oblivion. For four years, from 1933 to 1936, Colette spoke of all or almost all the plays put on in Paris and there is no need to say that, during those four years, we saw on the stage not only *Richard III* and *Coriolanus, La Machine Infernale* and *La Guerre de Troie n'Aura pas Lieu,* but many dramas and comedies of which we have forgotten even the title, even the name of the author, as well as cabaret shows, sumptuous and futile revues, and all the most mediocre, most frivolous and most

ephemeral things that show business can offer to its 'customers.' It is therefore admirable that everything which is,
by its very nature, or by its lack of quality, without a future,
should be provided with a future by the commentary which
is made on it, that criticism can ensure a sort of duration in
the memory of men to the very thing which it condemns,
by the form itself in which it condemns it, and that it can
after twelve years interest us, in a manner as immediate and
lively as this, in what it says about something which itself
interests us no longer. . . ."

Yes, but this is a very rare privilege. Usually the criticisms
are lost and the works remain. The only examples I can
think of that invalidate that aphorism are the *Salons* of
Diderot and those of Baudelaire, and they are concerned
with painting and not dramatic art.

In that brilliant, incisive and easy manner which is habitual with him, Thierry Maulnier goes on to develop this
assumption of his: that it is perhaps in those chronicles that
Colette's essential qualities are best combined. I cannot resist the temptation to copy to the end those pages devoted
to *La Jumelle Noire*:

"Of all the dramatic critics Colette is perhaps the only one
who is equally at home in those three worlds, separate and
yet linked by their close dependence on each other, the
worlds of the Back-stage, the Stage, and the Auditorium. She
alone is able to observe with the same fraternal eye, and the
penetration that comes from an all-embracing sympathy, the
sleep of an exhausted little girl, who is like a tired young
animal, and the secret of how a great writer, faced with an
empty page, sets to work. And finally she alone unites the
utmost swiftness in those varied steps by which the mind iso-

lates significant details, to enable it to take hold of them, with her power of making us see, hear and touch the whole, and bringing to life for us at the same time as the movement of the action, the significance of a theme, the meanderings of a plot, the play of light on a face and the quivering fold of a drapery. And I must not forget how she combines with that severe precision of look and pen a sort of fraternal affection for the work, for the effort, for the constant struggle of man and woman against all the uncertainty and imperfection that every form of work and of life entail, a fundamental kindness without which a critic can neither feel nor understand. There is no true criticism without charity."

Views on a work which I myself rate so highly and on which it would be my greatest pleasure to enlarge, I am in general obliged to deny myself. Everything that others may know or discover without me has no place here. My object is to show a woman in her activities and her repose, and as much through the things in which she resembles ordinary people as in those which distinguish her from them, since the detail of her life is important to those who love her work. My task is to reconcile the woman who, from the edge of her box, pierced with the most penetrating look possible the secrets of theatrical illusion, the woman who, in turn chronicler of the theatre and of fashion, judicial reporter, even columnist, unfailingly brought out the hidden meaning of what is ephemeral, misused, doomed to mere show, and the countrywoman passionately intent on the essential mysteries of life. Colette's lucid investigation of dressing-rooms and back-stage, as of the hidden side of the human heart, had its own source in the very sources which she so eagerly scrutinised. But the page we have just read reveals in its author so great a perspicacity concerning the springs of action in Colette, such an instinctive awareness of what went to make up her profound humanity, that it encroaches on my enterprise, so much so that I could not pass it over in silence.

# XIV

I KNEW WELL ENOUGH of Colette's need to get away from Paris as often as possible. In the summer we used to spend a good two months at Saint-Tropez. In winter and spring we had to make do with week ends. It was nearly always the Forest of Rambouillet which attracted us. We knew its smallest paths. "Everything that people say of a forest is true or becomes so. But it must be a very big forest, vast enough to reabsorb into itself at dawn its nocturnal secrets, as well as its fringe of wild beasts which range outside its borders during the night."

She sometimes said that what takes place in a forest does not entirely concern us. For that reason she always walked there with caution, rustling the dry leaves as little as possible, her ear suddenly alert, on the look-out for tracks, footprints, droppings, seeing more than was visible. We would go and hunt for the first anemones, the first bluebells; we used to leave Paris at dawn to gather lilies of the valley. One day when I was walking rather far behind Colette, I saw her wave away with an imperious gesture the bulldog Souci, who began to limp, as was her habit whenever she had a guilty thought. As soon as I caught up with Colette I found her on her knees, signing to me to make no noise as I drew near. Lying flat on the ground, among the pale green leaves of the lily of the valley, there was a nest on which sat a hen-pheasant hatching her eggs. In the face of that dog which she had seen approaching, and of her most redoubtable enemy, man, bending over her, she remained motionless, dominating her panic fear and resisting her instinct to flee, heroically await- ing death rather than abandon her eggs. Her delicate head erect, one could see her breast palpitating with anguish and her little body trembling in its tawny plumage. Her hands apart, Colette was whispering to her in a sort of cooing lan- guage, which for all we can know was perhaps her own, and trembling just as much as the bird.

When I am asked occasionally whether Colette ever ex- perienced metaphysical anguish, or anxiety as to the future of mankind, whether she ever sought God beyond his crea- tures or found a refuge in prayer, I should like to answer by showing her in a scene such as that or any other of the same kind, quivering with pity and fervour, one with everything that lives and breathes.

But one must not confuse Colette's ardour for discover- ing the world, her passionate absorption in creatures and things with any kind of blind joy of living. I do not believe that to penetrate ever more deeply into nature and her wiles makes one very optimistic. Behind her enthusiasm Colette was grave. There is no respect without gravity. Capable, thank God, of childishness, but not at all frivolous. Frivolity is the prerogative of the male: he has not experienced the mystery of life in his own body.

But to join forces with everything that is born, grows,

prospers and declines and can only do so at the price of crime, means adopting innocence as a principle. Then what are we to do about that distribution of sufferings and rewards proposed in the name of a morality which everything one observes contradicts? How can we persuade ourselves that we ought to devote our days to the search for an unknowable abstraction, when there awaits our knowledge all that swarms in the grass at our feet, in the bark of dead tree-trunks, all that buds and thrusts forward towards life? What is that salvation of our souls which we are urged to consider, while so many remain in need of help, what are these vain ecstasies, what have we to repent of? And, finally, what remains of the greatness of man if one takes from him his solitude, his awareness of his ephemeral state, his disinterested effort?

I am only putting myself forward here, with the very greatest precaution. I do not deny that it is risky, perhaps hardly honest, however well one may have known someone, to interpret them thus in the most private of their beliefs. I add that I was not master of Colette's hours of meditation as she sat at her tapestry, that we respected long and trustful silences between ourselves, and that we did not think that first causes were a subject of conversation. The fact remains that I owe the public, in such measure as I am responsible to it, and in spite of the fragile nature of it, my testimony as to what lay at the root of Colette's behaviour and was therefore the foundation of her work.

# XV

PHILIPPE DE ROTHSCHILD has just telephoned me to know if I possess a copy of *Lac aux Dames,* the film whose production he directed in 1933, and for which Colette wrote the dialogue. He reminded me how remarkable this was and asserted that it was largely responsible for the world success of the film. Colette also wrote the dialogue of *Jeunes Filles en Uniforme* and the success of that, too, was great. Colette's famous style had no part in this, since dialogue for the theatre or the cinema is no good if it does not know how to divest itself of the ornaments of writing. It has to hit the right tone, to be direct, and above all to see to it that each person speaks throughout in character. Was this therefore a *tour de force* on the part of Colette, a spontaneous adaptation to a craft new to her? Hardly, for if one examines the dialogues in her novels and stories more closely, one sees that they could not be more natural and that it was merely the richness of the context which prevented one from realising this at the start. The dialogues in *Chérie* and *Gigi* were transferred from the novel to the play or the film without needing a word changed. Perhaps too much has been said of Colette's miraculous instinct. It does not explain every-thing. Choice is before everything else a question of intelli-gence, and there was no moment when Colette was not exer-cising choice with the utmost strictness.

Even so, if anyone had denied her intelligence, Colette would not have taken exception to that. Just the reverse of Madame de Noailles, who was always ostentatiously laying claim to it. I found myself, one evening, sitting on her right at dinner in the house of Countess Amélie Murat, a poetess when the mood was on her. Everyone knows how inexhaus-tible and dazzling was the conversation of Madame de Noailles, or rather her monologue, full of parentheses and twists and turns, all glittering with images. But hardly had she sat down than Madame Murat began to speak and, being at least as voluble as Madame de Noailles and endowed with a much more powerful voice, she crushed all the latter's at-tempts to join in. Sensing her opportunity, and under cover of fulsome praises, she made the comment that Madame de Noailles would find most disagreeable:

"You are not intelligent, my dear Anna, and you have no need to be. Your genius makes up for everything. . . ."

"I," answered Madame de Noailles—but I was the only one who could hear it—"I, who am the most intelligent woman of the century!"

"You have only to listen to the voices which inspire you. . . . What use would intelligence be to you?"

"I, who—" But the voice of Madame de Noailles was lost amid the clarion calls booming down the table.

Finally a little cough forced Countess Murat to interrupt herself for an instant, and Madame de Noailles leapt into the breach with these words which she brought out at the top of her voice:

"I must speak or die!"

Our relations with Philippe de Rothschild had been formed on the *Eros*, a yacht belonging to his father, Baron Henri de Rothschild, who invited us in 1930 for a cruise in the fjords of Norway. Dr. Henri de Rothschild was a curious man who had genuinely studied medicine, was a genuine dramatic author under the name of André Pascal and was continually branching out in all directions. Timid by nature, with a desperate need of sympathy and warmth, he carried his wealth like a curse, for it bred a worm in all his plans even before they came to fruition, and instilled suspicion in the least of his human relations. In a word, he would have given his fortune to be poor, which seems easy, but at the same time he would have had to go on living his life in his own way, and so he would have had to buy poverty, like any other commodity.

The *Eros*, a thousand tonner, was one of the most beautiful yachts of the day. She required a crew of thirty-three and had room for twenty guests. From the moment of leaving Paris to the home port, either on board or at the ports of call, it was impossible for the guests to spend the slightest thing, unless they had thrown banknotes into the sea, and even then I am sure the notes would have been fished out for them. And yet no one found the management of money more difficult than did Henri de Rothschild. He would in turn find an expenditure of three million reasonable, or object to an outlay of a hundred francs, not out of avarice but from a congenital ignorance of the relative value of things.

He had given us an example of this the year before. Since we had ten days for our Easter holidays, Colette and I had organised a little trip. The upshot of this story will, I fear, make the word organise seem a little ambitious. As our destination was Tangiers, we decided to go through Spain in order to visit the Goyas in their own home in Madrid. Everything went well as far as Madrid, which we reached by rail. We had merely omitted to find out if the Prado was open: because of Easter Week it wasn't. Farewell, Goya! Neither had we reserved our places in the train from Madrid to Seville and Algeciras: because of Holy Week there was not one free. We had a parley with a taxi which looked all right and which agreed to transport us. It was a delicious journey which took us from La Mancha, still bleak and nipping under its cold light, to meet the suave and blossoming spring of Andalusia. We stayed at Seville long enough for one or two processions and a few popular dances. It so happened that we were never able to give ourselves enough leisure to linger anywhere, so that Colette, great reader of travel books though she was, knew better the countries where she had not been than those she had visited. She could discuss the details of some Guatemalan puebla or some Hindoo temple, but we had only been able to give two days to New York and three to the whole of Spain.

At Algeciras a good hotel of the high-tea kind, kept by some English women, with a patio and border of pansies; then the crossing as far as Ceuta in a doubtful-looking old tub; and finally Tangiers. We stayed at the hotel, but the Glaoui, Pasha of Marrakech, who has just died, and who always expressed a deferential friendship for Colette, had put at our disposal one of his properties so that we might wander in the vast gardens crammed with nightingales, where all the rarest kinds of trees grew in dense confusion. Arum lilies, a luxury-flower in Paris, were weeds here, the livid velvet of their cornets thrusting up everywhere.

Hardly had we arrived than we had to leave. I reserved cabins on a Dutch ship, which called at Gibraltar and Toulon en route for the Dutch Indies. Gibraltar with its sugar-loaf rock, its English soldiers, tall, blond, spick-and-span, circulating among the short dark Spaniards, pleased Colette. The first person who we met there was Henri de Rothschild, whose yacht was anchored in the roads and who invited us to dinner that same evening.

It was our first contact with the *Eros*. At table the Baron made us tell him of our journey. All of a sudden, stupefaction was stamped on his face:

"You say you took a taxi from Madrid to Algeciras?"

"Yes, of course we did."

"But . . . but . . . how much did it cost you?"

Colette, who did not know, turned to me:

"Nine thousand five hundred pesetas," I said.

"Nine thousand five hundred pesetas! But it's madness!"

"Why?" interrupted Colette. "Since we happened to have them for once. . . ."

The Baron, who had just spent twenty-two million 1929 francs on his brand-new boat, took his head in his two hands and called his daughter to witness our crazy statements. We were told that he talked of it long afterwards. To understand something of the ideas of multi-millionaires where money is concerned one would have to become a multi-millionaire oneself, and that is really too tiring.

The *Eros* was therefore known to us when we embarked

at Le Havre for the northern waters. Colette loved the sea, although she had discovered it late. She loved being before, in and on it, in spite of sea-sickness which she had very readily, if one may put it that way.

We had not gone far when we ran into a heavy swell over the Dogger Bank, and this sent the guests to their cabins to meditate on the fact that a big yacht is never anything but a little boat. Only the Captain and I . . . for once it was true, except that I am not sure about the Captain.

As the swell continued to increase, the ship almost ceased to make headway, so instead of going directly to Norway with Bergen as our first port of call, it was decided to go via the Kiel Canal, Copenhagen and the Skagerrak. One by one we saw the passengers reappearing on the deck, looking a little vague and with wavering smiles.

The couple on board whom we knew best were the Léopold Marchands. Colette had known them longer than I had. As is known, Léopold Marchand collaborated with her in the plays which she adapted from *Chéri* and *La Vagabonde,* one in 1921 and the other in 1923. He was an amiable man, very tall and bulky, with a rosy, heavy-jowled face, pince-nez on his nose. Full of fun, he had the most courteous manners in the world, and had never consented to call Colette, for whom he felt a boundless admiration, anything but "Madame." His wife, a ravishing Pole, who had been the first wife of Alfred Savoir, contrived to be a Jewess in spite of having the most beautiful blue eyes, fair hair and a little turned-up Parisian nose. She was exquisite in every way and Colette loved her with a great protective tenderness. When the war came, the Polish family of "Miche," as everyone called her, was decimated and ruined. She tried to put a

brave face on it, but the loss of her own folk made her more
sensitive still to the miserable lot of so many people tracked
down by the war, and she could not get them out of her
mind. In addition she imagined that, being a Jewess, she
risked becoming an embarrassment to her husband, whom
she adored. So in order not to cause him embarrassment, she
caused him despair. One evening Léopold Marchand found
her lifeless in her bath, having taken enough sleeping tablets
to kill her.

The almost total absence of night at Trondheim in Norway where we arrived on Midsummer Day, and the unexpected position of the sun in the sky "offended" Colette, as
she wrote to a friend. "I'm having trouble with the sun,"
she added, "it's never in the place where it should be."

She had inherited from Sido a concern for the cardinal
points. When she was travelling she always had to get her
bearings, to know where the sun rose and set, and what
were the prevailing winds. The same at home in Paris, it
goes without saying. But does it in fact go without saying?

"I have just been visiting so and so," she said to me one
day. "Ah, I'm not at all satisfied."

"Why? What's wrong?"

"Nothing . . . her health . . . her household."

"What did you advise her?"

"Why, to move house, of course!"

"Why?"

"Haven't you noticed that her apartment faces north-east?
How could anything good happen to her with such an
aspect?"

"What did she answer?"

"Just you wait, this really beats everything. She asked me

how I knew that her flat faces north-east. Because she herself knew nothing about it. And she's been living in that
house for twelve years. Really, Maurice, can you understand
that?"

"No, I confess I can't, for it so happens that I do pay attention to this matter. I know in the morning when I open my
eyes whether the wind is from the west or the east. When it's
from the east I feel happier in my skin."

"Like all other cats," she remarked, "when the wind is
from the east they dance. With me, it's just the opposite, I
love humidity, as you know. No doubt it's necessary for my
lungs and my temperament, or perhaps it merely satisfies
something vegetable in me. But you can't imagine the
number of people who are absolutely ignorant about themselves: it's like ships without a compass. Can you possibly
understand that anyone should go drifting about like that,
not attached to anything?"

As she got on in life, she needed more instruments of control, as if navigation were becoming more difficult. In the
end, she had around her divan-raft a barometer, an outdoor
thermometer, which she could consult from where she lay,
compasses, a number of watches, chronometers, binoculars,
and magnifying glasses.

On our return, the proprietor of the *Eros* decided to call
at Amsterdam. To do that you have to leave the North Sea
and cross Northern Holland by the Ymuiden Canal. So our
boat entered the canal and we . . . *descended* towards the
land. I saw Colette open-mouthed. This unaccustomed
manoeuvre upset all her innate and acquired ideas on the
proper relations between land and sea. Now we were gliding
through the canal and there were the fields, lower than our-

selves, with peasants moving about on them. Colette raised her arms to heaven:

"But it's madness!" she cried. "Those good people are running the greatest danger. They can't know anything about it. We must warn them at once!"

I reassured her:

"You can see from here that it's all held by the dykes!"

"Yes, but if at any moment a little boy, playing with a little stick, made a little hole in the dyke, there would be no more Holland."

Her instinct was not so far wrong. It is, alas, what sometimes happens . . . nearly.

# XVI

WE ARE STILL vainly searching for the script of *Lac aux Dames* and all chances of finding it seem exhausted. As a last resort one might turn on the sound-track and take down the words. Thus it is that to-day writings sometimes disappear, but thanks to pictures, words remain.

Colette had written for *Lac aux Dames* a very pretty song. I have kept that. For fear that in its turn it too may disappear in smoke, here it is:

### The Further Bank

On the further bank
I wait and sing.
The lake rocks
My dream, but what
Will my bark bring
At evening, or dawn?
Far off there gleam
The lights of the fête . . .
Here in the shadow,
Cleaving the green water,
Drip from my oar
Drops of the moon.

From the further bank
He comes!
O handsome youth
Risen from the lake,
Battered by the wind
Drenched by the rain!
Fair son of the day
Cast by the night
Into my boat!
Here in the shadow
Your body is drenched
With drops of the moon . . .
Towards the further bank
The lights of the fête
And the fair-haired girl
Have led him.
The lake that reflected
Our two faces
Mouth pressed to mouth
Now mirrors alone
My mouth that sings,
My eyes which stream
With tears? No, no, with
Drops of the moon . . .

On the *Eros*, in spite of the distractions which every hour offered, Colette worked every day. The book which she then had on the stocks was *Ces Plaisirs*. In addition she was taking notes (which she sometimes did on a journey though never in Paris), notes which are to be found in *En Pays Connu*, along with others, on our glissade across Spain.

Later on, when she was responsible for the theatre column of *Le Journal*, the annual closing of the theatres might have allowed her to take things a bit easy. She did nothing of the sort; a chronicle from Provence took the place in the holidays of the theatrical bulletin. These chronicles are to be found scattered through several works, in particular in *Journal à Rebours* and in *Belles Saisons*. This is a pity, for a collection of them would make a very attractive book on Provence.

How can one reconcile such constant labour with Colette's declared repugnance for her work as a writer? Was it love of money which drove her? Love of money, no, the fear of lacking it, yes, to some extent. On several occasions she was terribly short of it and such times of need leave traces. She had never been able to forget that her parents had been ruined to the point where their furniture was sold at auction in front of the door of the house where she was born. They had to leave Saint-Sauveur and take refuge at Chatillon-Coligny in the Loiret, in the house of Achille Robineau, Colette's elder half-brother, who tried to keep them all by means of his exhausting profession of a country doctor.

This ruin was the result of a dark peasant plot, slowly and tortuously hatched. When Sido married the Captain she was rich in lands and farms. The Captain undertook to see that they prospered. It would have been impossible to imagine a southern husband at that time leaving such matters to his wife to deal with. The Captain was a dreamer, full of charm, but good for little except war, and there is not always one of these on hand; besides, you can't wage war with only one leg. His farmers quickly grasped that he was weak and staggeringly ignorant where matters of breeding and crops were concerned. They embroiled him in extravagant repairs and expenditures. By chance there were money-lenders on the spot, ready to help, although at a rate of interest which might well have made him uneasy. These providential lenders were none other than our good farmers themselves, acting through middle-men; and by some mechanism of which I am ignorant and which I would in any case spare you, they woke up one fine day to find themselves proprietors of their farms and creditors of the Colettes into the bargain.

As a matter of fact the desire to earn money was at first an excuse which she gave herself in order not to recognise that she had ended by finding in writing, if not a pleasure, at least the satisfaction of winning a victory over herself.

"I never see you smoking any longer," I said one day.

"No. I noticed that I was beginning to enjoy it, so I began to be distrustful!"

I could give more than one example of this austerity. Near the end of her life she sometimes rang for Pauline:

"Pauline, I must work. Give me some paper."

"Madame would do much better to rest. Why does Madame want to write?"

"Why, Pauline, because it's my job."

I hope I am showing Colette sufficiently in the freedom of her acts, the independence of her judgment, and her bold humanity not to feel obliged to keep silent on her virtues which, incidentally, are written in every line of her work. Others might prefer her entirely given up to her instincts, free of all discipline, unbridled, in short. I would be glad enough to agree to that, but in that case how explain those fifty books, on every page of which she exercised, every day, the strictest control?

# XVII

IT IS VERY DIFFICULT for a speech on admission to an academy to be anything other than a rather cold piece of oratory. Colette had felt a real satisfaction at her nomination to the Belgian Academy of French Language and Literature, but the prospect of the discourse to be composed cast a shadow over her days.

"I'll never get the hang of a thing like that," she had said. After which she took up her pen and found at the first attempt the right tone. But that is for others to say.

If the word of an employee of the Belgian Sûreté had been taken the discourse would never have been pronounced. We had not paid any attention to the fact that Colette's passport was out of date, and this model functionary was set on making her get out of the train which was taking us to Brussels just in time for the session, in order to send her back. We had with us the Princess Edmond de Polignac, a great friend of the arts and of artists, who added to an American accent a way of speaking with her jaw thrust forward, and practically without moving her lips, which produced a curious effect. With cold indignation she intervened:

"Your academy is expecting Madame for a discourse, and they can't begin without her."

This statement, which for him had no meaning, and the strange pronunciation, only strengthened the employee's determination. Colette did not say a word. She had been a prey since the evening before to stage-fright out of all proportion and I saw a mad hope spring up in her eyes: Providence was intervening, the session would not take place.

"I tell you that the passport is not in order," insisted the employee.

"And I tell you that without Madame there will be no discourse," repeated the Princess, her teeth more and more tightly clenched.

Finally the employee went off to consult someone, perhaps a superior, perhaps the cook on the train; whatever it was he gave in.

The Belgians have always given Colette the warmest of welcomes. Once again they showed her the greatest kindness and warmth. Her reception created a great deal of interest and the hall of the Palais des Académies was full to bursting.

Sitting in the front row, I watched Colette during the discourse of Valère Gille, which preceded hers, and I knew that, racked with fear and anxiety, she was longing for the end of the world. Yet when she stood up, very straight in a simple black frock that reached to the ground, her voice was firm, the hands that held the sheets of her discourse did not tremble at all and she gave a model reading. Once again, she had, as she used to say, "taken the plunge."

That same year 1936 saw the appearance of *Mes Appren-tissages,* which tells the story of Colette's life at the time of the Claudine books. Why that book, so entirely outside the time that we were living through together? It was because its hour had come. Between Colette's childhood and *La Maison de Claudine,* followed by *Sido,* there is about the same interval as between her life as a young woman and *Mes Apprentissages.* Colette's work follows a strict order without her having ever taken the least trouble to give it a design. She merely thought she was keeping, one after the other, the promises she had made to periodicals and pub-lishers. "I haven't got a subject," she would groan, "I never have had a subject." "Haven't you got a subject for me?" she would sometimes ask a visitor, whoever he might be, and who would remain speechless.

She always made me read what she was writing as she went along. I used to take great care in giving her my ad-vice. Not for fear of wounding her, but, on the contrary, because her humility, where her work was concerned, was so great that at the least reserve on my part she wanted to begin all over again. I risked seeing the pages which she had submitted to me torn up before I had time to prevent her doing so.

Those years between 1932–33 and the war are years of fullness and peaceful happiness about which I have very little to say. The days overlapped without shock or grating, devoted to work, to some friendships and above all to the pleasure we had in being together. An attachment such as this, whose roots every day grow deeper and become more entwined, prevents one from knowing that, each day, time with an invisible hand is carving a line on a face, shortening the breath, making the footstep heavier. Was it in 1937 or was it in 1938 while walking behind Colette, whose step was still rapid, that I first noticed that slight crookedness of the hip? Was it in 1938 or 1939 that she said for the first time: "My goodness, my right hip is hurting me"?

However she was still a good walker when, in 1938, *Paris-Soir* sent us both to Fez to follow the sessions of a sensational trial. Some children who were playing on a piece of vacant land had found a heavy hamper out of which, hardly had they touched it, there rolled a head and some human limbs, the whole of it carefully boiled down. The police soon discovered where this macabre decoction had come from: the house of prostitution of Oum-el Hassen, called Moulay Hassen. When they began looking into the matter more closely they found that three other prostitutes had disappeared from that hospitable house recently, and four had died. In the course of the search, a faint noise was heard behind a wall. When it was broken open the wall revealed four little girls and a boy of fifteen in the last stages of starvation and showing the marks of various tortures.

Moulay Hassen, a woman of fifty, had herself been a prostitute famous throughout the whole of Morocco, not only for her beauty but for her heroic attitude on behalf of the French at the time of the conquest. There was talk of great services rendered, and illustrious friendships.

In all this there was the possibility of evoking a whole past, with gallops through the golden dust of sunsets, reported in contrast to a sordid crime whose horror had rarely been equalled, and a mysterious woman who resembled both Antinea and Bluebeard: a fine trial if ever there was

one. Colette was to give impressions of the sessions and I
a technical account of the cross examinations.

We took the train for Toulouse, for at that time the
Moroccan planes did not leave from Paris. They were Laté-
coères which called at Barcelona and Oran before landing
at Casablanca. At Barcelona one could hear in the distance
the guns of the Spanish war.

Hardly had we arrived at Fez than we rushed to see the
counsel of Oum-el Hassen, a Frenchman from Toulouse. He
seemed very flattered to receive us.

"To what do I owe the honour of your visit?"

"We have been sent by *Paris-Soir* to cover the trial."

"What trial?"

"What do you mean, what trial? Why, the trial of Moulay Hassen, of course!"

"Indeed! And you bothered to come from Paris for that?"

"For that? But it's an unheard-of affair, come now!"

"No, no, no—you've been misled. *It's only to do with
women*. It isn't even known within one or two how many
there are and it never will be known. They are mountain
women, who haven't even got any civil status. A crime? Oh!
yes, of course, of course! But still, if there hadn't been that
hamper! A few women more or less! Nobody here pays any
attention."

We soon learnt that this contempt might have been explained by a dislike for women, particular to our barrister
who was reputed to find the company of young legionaries
more attractive. But everyone assured us that we had been
the victims of a misunderstanding. If there was a crowd at
the trial it was rather to see Colette and the other few
French journalists who were present. As for the heroic past

and the illustrious friendships, they were conveniently conjured away.

In the Court where everyone knew each other there
reigned a good-natured atmosphere. In the course of his
pleading the barrister from Toulouse suddenly cried, wav-
ing his sleeves dramatically: "It's as though one were to
pretend, gentlemen, that I frequent the legionaries! . . .
Well, it may be true, but all the same it must be proved!"

This bravado, which was customary with him, only
brought a discreet smile to the faces of the audience.

Oum-el Hassen got off with fifteen years of forced labour.
After all it was only to do with women!

In the long run, what remains of this trial is the account
which Colette gave of it and which is to be found in *Journal
à Rebours*.


"Don't you think we've played with the Rue de Marignan
long enough?" she said to me one fine day.

I did think so, all the more because I'd never really taken
part in the game, not considering the cultivation of strawberries in Paris a very exciting pastime.

The Marignan building, now that all its offices were let,
resounded all day long with the banging of doors and the
whirring of lifts. At night, on the other hand, and on Sundays, it turned into a disquieting desert. But above all the
Champs Elysées is not a real district. Colette always looked
for a province in Paris and it is so easy to find one there.
Four streets crossing in a particular way, and you have a
clannish feeling, a conformity, a style, I almost said an ethic.
It was time to find a concierge somewhere, instead of a

porter, jointly owned cats, a smiling dairy woman, a bantering butcher.

Even at that time it was not too easy to find a place to live in Paris. Colette fixed "our" choice on a flat under the roof in a corner of the Place Vendôme. The view of the Place was beautiful, in spite of the architectural and historical heresy represented by the column. But it looked as if it would be difficult to make much of the flat, which was three-quarters hidden behind a pediment, and I well knew that once again it was this challenge which had attracted Colette. But why should I have deprived her, by dissuading her from it, of setting out on another flight of fancy, which even if it let her down, could have as its worst consequence only another move?

However, Providence was watching over her, in the shape of a journalist and dramatic author called Arnyvelde. He wanted an interview and he was not the only one. Colette was working and he was twice shown the door. But the agents of destiny are tenacious too, and finally Arnyvelde was received.

"I know, Madame," he said incautiously, "that you are going to move, and they say you like nothing better than moving house."

"What!" burst out Colette, quite untruthfully. "Those who say that lie in their throats. In the first place I've so far moved house only fourteen times, and each time it was because I was absolutely obliged to. The proof of that is that when, ten years ago, I lived in the Palais Royal, I went down on my hands and knees to try and rent the first floor of my house, and if I had been able to get it I should never have moved again."

This declaration appeared, just as it stood, in *Paris-Midi* a few days later. The next day Colette received a letter:

"Madam: I read in *Paris-Midi* that you still hanker after the first floor of 9 Rue de Beaujolais. I am living in this flat and I am quite ready to give it up to you. . . ."

Even at that time this was fantastic enough; to-day it would seem sheer lunacy. The Place Vendôme, of course, crumbled into dust and thus began our link with the Palais Royal which has meant so much for us.

# XVIII

S HE READ a great deal and with surprising rapidity, yet
without ever skipping a line, and with attention too, as
in everything that she did. From time to time she would un-
screw her pen and correct a printer's error, out of habit and
without being aware of it. Balzac and Proust were the authors whom she re-read untiringly. She also loved novels of
action, tales of the sea or with an exotic atmosphere, and
had read in their French translations all of Kipling and
Conrad.

By chance I was present each time that she received new
volumes of Proust, since *Albertine Disparue* and *Le Temps
Retrouvé* appeared after 1925. She left what she was doing
and without losing a minute began to read with brooding
attention. Her taste for Proust dated from the first lines of
*Du Côté de Chez Swann.*

The twenty volumes of Balzac in the Houssiaux edition,
with their backs of grained red leather, were always within
reach of her hand. She would choose a volume at random
and knew her way in them so well that she could say what
had gone before and what was to follow. Balzac was for her

a world whose characters and houses were all familiar to her.

She had a different method with Proust. She re-read him every two years more or less, giving herself up to him as to a wave. "I go in at one end," she used to say, "and come out at the other." But she never read him piecemeal.

Proust, on his side, admired Colette. The letters which he addressed to her have not got that tone of worldly toady-ism habitual with him, and thereby they mark his esteem. Colette and he met occasionally and Colette has composed two striking portraits of him.

Colette was often asked to undertake a literary column but she always resisted this temptation, in the first place not to spoil her pleasure as a reader. "And besides," she would add, "I take no pleasure in making heads roll."

No interviewer succeeded in making her judge her con-temporaries; I in my turn shall be silent about them too.

Stendhal hardly moved her at all. She sometimes made an effort to read him, but could never work up any enthusiasm. Their techniques were too different. She preferred Mérimée, if only for *La Vénus d'Ille.* She liked the plays of Musset, and particularly *Lorenzaccio,* which she knew by heart. We went one evening to see a revival of this play at the Comédie Française, from the box of the administrator who at that time was Emile Fabre. They had "lightened" the work by means of some important cuts. Colette of course noticed this and was choking with an indignation she could barely re-strain when Monsieur Fabre, the man responsible, turning towards her and another dramatic writer present in the box, said with a note of triumph, in which was apparent an ancient grudge against those spoilsports that living authors are:

"Well? You see what can be done with a dead writer!"

Even when she was young, Alexandre Dumas was never able to attract her. The only thing which could wean her away from authenticity was a certain poetic romanticism, and in Dumas she found neither the one nor the other. She had a weakness for Flaubert's *Salammbô* and preferred *l'Education Sentimentale* to *Madame Bovary*. The Fromentin she liked was the author of *Voyage au Sahel, Un Été Dans le Sahara,* and even *Les Maîtres d'Autrefois* rather than the author of *Dominique*.

She had read Alphonse Daudet from her childhood, with a preference for *Fromont Jeune et Risler Aîné,* and *Le Nabab*. She appreciated Zola, especially *l'Assommoir*. She reproached Anatole France with always avoiding the difficulty.

"He proceeds by cuts and abstentions. I see too clearly how it's done," she used to say.

Shakespeare she enjoyed, in the translation by François-Victor Hugo, although not all Shakespeare. About 1937 the famous Austrian producer, Max Reinhardt, asked Colette to make a new adaptation of *A Midsummer Night's Dream,* which he would have put on in Paris. He did not carry out his plan because he could not find the necessary financial backing. It is a pity: Colette would have felt quite at home in the Shakespearian forest, and Bottom and Puck would have called forth her tenderest care.

She read and re-read Edgar Allan Poe in Baudelaire's translation. She was sensitive to all poetry, particularly Ver-

laine's, although she did describe him as "an old trickster."
She liked Leconte de Lisle for the same reasons as she
liked *Salammbô:* a verbal richness allied to a bad taste so
shattering as to become pleasant. She was hard on Mallarmé,
though she enjoyed his verbal games.

Close though she sometimes was to Montaigne by her
turn of mind, and to the great authors of the seventeenth
century by the firmness of her language, she had not in
actual fact read them. Molière, yes, but who can resist
Molière?

Late in her life I revealed La Rochefoucauld to her, and
for a long time she kept a little copy of his *Maximes* on her
work-table. With Saint Simon I succeeded where Sido had
failed, Sido who had been astonished that at eight years her
daughter did not prize the *Mémoires.* She was also entranced
by the *Lettres de la Princesse Palatine,* in the edition which
I made for the Club du Livres Français, and she occasionally
asked me for them again.

She liked Courteline and Labiche, Jules Renard much
less.

She enjoyed popular scientific works in all their forms.
Also botany, natural history, life in the ocean depths, birds
and butterflies: Fabre's *Souvenirs Entomologiques,* Maeter-
linck, d'Orbigny's *Dictionnaire Universel d'Histoire Naturelle,* the *Annales de Flore, L'Horticulteur Universel,
Botanique* by Le Maout, *Lépidoptères* by Lucas, *A la Mer*
by G. Epy, the *Dictionnaire Pittoresque d'Histoire Naturelle*
by Guerin, a hundred works of the same kind.

And travel, ah! travels! The sixty-eight volumes of the
*Tour du Monde,* read from one end to the other several
times. Livingston, Stanley, Huc, Landon, Arago, Comte de

Beauvoir, Schweinfurth, Madame Ida Pfeifer, and so many others.

She often used the word "style," but never in the sense of a manner of writing. She would speak of the style of a man, an animal, or a thing, to express how that man, animal, or thing conformed to a species in its movement and bearing. That swift, sharp glance, which filled with astonishment all those who were subjected to it, not only took in straight off all the details of what she was looking at, but also assigned a category to it. That is why whatever she described, although she imagined that only the particular ever concerned her, so easily took on a universal value.

As an example of this I would like to quote a piece called *Serpents* which figures in *Prisons et Paradis:*

"A hundred and twenty, a hundred and sixty pounds of serpent on the low fork of a dead tree. Nothing in the cage seems alive. Will that dead branch be the first to move? Polished, glazed, oiled by generations of reptiles, cylindrical, undulating, and here and there swollen . . . Perhaps it was the branch which ate a rabbit last week?"

From the very first words we have penetrated into the reptilian universe, in which even the inanimate participates.

"On the high fork sleeps, or appears to sleep, a hundred-weight of python. Coiled in a spiral in the first place, he has subsequently made sure of his equilibrium by looping himself into a 'figure of eight,' like a skein. But what to do with the ten feet still hanging down? He has drawn up this remnant in a casual way and has secured it by half hitches and weaver's knots and concealed the end. Two transparent rags, two nets in coarse meshed, spider-coloured tulle, bear witness that the spring has unsheathed the two great serpents. They are new. A stream, a chromium-plated weapon gleam less than they do. But where is the neck, the flank, the head? These cylinders, oppressed by their own weight, are clad in a paving of enamel. The back and the flanks— if those are the flanks and back—display the blue of the swallow, the yellow green of the willow, two or three browns like newly varnished pottery and as many beiges set out in the simplest of mosaic patterns. And I say ingenuously: 'The artlessness of these designs,' just at the very moment when I perceive that at one point the little scaly triangles, here in squares and there drawn out into lozenges or crushed in a trapezium, form a kind of eye, an orb almost endowed with a dead look, and I draw back. . . . That creature, which hides its end and its beginning, which watches and terrifies with its back, and I, we come neither from the same country nor from the same belly. . . ."

There is what distinguishes the motionless serpent from everything else in the world. Now it must be made to move in its own way, which cannot be confused with anything.

"To resume. In here one breathes a sickly smell of half-dried puddles, unfamiliar excrements, a sweet and greenish air which enervates the heart. . . . Hardly had I thought 'motionless' than the walls of the cage, its muddy pool and the ground on which I stand, shift all together with a well-coordinated impetus for a few seconds, the space of a dream —one does not measure the duration of a cataclysm. . . . Once again everything reels and glides horribly—I feel no jerk but a sickly tilting accompanied by a convex distortion. . . . It is the python that has moved, the python I had thought immovable—we must beware of this word, beware: let us make a little detour and leave it there—and which has begun to move, drawing along with it my surprised senses, my limited eyes accustomed to paws and leaps and governed by the logic of steps.

"It moves: thus does the tide advance upon the long sands, the tide that depends upon the moon. Thus does poison glide along the veins, and thus evil in the mind. I might still hope that it is not moving if the oily light clinging to it were not passing over its knots with a harmony that dismays. It moves and goes nowhere. It has released neither its head nor its tail. It melts into itself, begins again, progresses but does not change place, reabsorbs and dilates itself without uncoiling.

"It moves and the solid universe capsizes. Can it be that, from the very first serpent of the world, man has fluctuated and reeled under a serpent's weight?"

I had not intended to go in for literary criticism here. Yet as soon as I try and explain Colette's use of a word, I get drawn into it. But perhaps the key word to her is "style." Colette restores to us not only the object but its "style" as well, that is to say, its poetic dimension.

See how this serpent, from the very first lines, becomes *the* serpent, the serpent species, then an idea, a serpent-abstraction, a world the reverse of our own. The invincible aversion of man, of western man at least, and of all animals to the serpent finds itself finally justified in that phrase: "It moves and the solid universe capsizes."

"Sickly smell of puddles," "sweet and greenish air," "sickly tilting," the "walls of the cage, its muddy pool and the ground on which I stand, shift all together," no one has ever been able to read this piece in public for fear of provoking nausea and giddiness. And the phrase: "It melts into itself, begins again, progresses but does not change place, reabsorbs and dilates itself without uncoiling," has not this the very movement of the serpent?

Why should I not marvel as much as anyone else at this sovereign art? Will people say that it is not my subject? And yet if I want to give the truest possible picture of Colette, I shall not succeed by stringing anecdotes together, by showing her only in her daily life. There were not two persons in her and no writer has been on more intimate terms with his work. Certainly the oxygen of the heights is not an air that one can breathe and there was no question of it between us; but whether she liked it or not, Colette could not help threads of gold weaving themselves into the warp of her days. Occupied by the cares of her household and her job, she remained a poet. The mode, not the music, was different, the genius remained.

In order to write *Serpents* and some other portraits of animals, which served in the first place as a text for a book illustrated by Jouve, *Paradis Terrestres,* which appeared in 1932, Colette went to spend a day in the zoological garden at Antwerp. She brought back with her a short-lived friendship with some keepers of the wild beasts, and the melancholy which the sight of the caged animals had given her. She minded this less at the circus because there the animals end by becoming actors to a certain extent, with their routine, their rehearsals, and the waiting for their act, so boredom weighs upon them less.

It was in the course of that same year, I think, that we received an invitation from a big German travelling circus. Its owner, who was called Sarrasani, had about him something of the great nobleman, the oriental potentate, and the bear-leader, all at the same time. He would very much have liked to come to Paris, but could not get a licence for it, since apparently the French circuses were secretly and stubbornly opposed to him. In order to win over opinion, he had the idea of inviting eighteen French journalists to spend several days in Berlin, where the circus then was.

We arrived at Berlin in the morning. We were taken to the Hôtel Excelsior, one of the best in the city. It was early and the day promised to be a full one, so Colette and I decided to rest for a bit. Hardly had we dozed off than a terrifying din broke out in the hotel, a brazen uproar in which the trumpets of Jericho had apparently joined forces with those of the Last Judgment. It was Sarrasani's forty musicians, in the echoing vestibule of the Excelsior. Clad in scarlet, they were serenading us with their music, which claimed that it could set the canvas of the biggest possible tent flapping. The attention was delicate, the effect terrifying.

As soon as we had recovered from our emotion, they came to fetch us for our visit to the circus. We beheld a world of tents, lorries, and caravans covering an immense area. At the entrance to the big tent, the sumptuous Sarrasani was waiting for us, a handsome man, rather plump, with hieratic gestures, behind a counter. Two big round baskets in front of him held a recent harvest of lion and tiger cubs, only a few days old. As though he were offering us a flower to put in our buttonhole, Sarrasani proposed, with an affable smile: "A little lion, or would you rather have a little tiger?"

Colette and he were immediately the best of friends. Theatre and circus folk adored her spontaneously. The pride of Sarrasani was a troupe of eighteen superb elephants which he presented to the public himself, dressed as a Maharajah

in white silk covered with embroideries, his turban sur-
mounted by a white aigrette. With their heads touching the
canvas roof, they looked like monoliths left behind by a
civilisation of giants. When Colette exclaimed at their
healthy appearance, Sarrasani said to her majestically: "Madame, they shall be in front of your hotel tomorrow morning to wish you good day." He would have kept his word—
we learned later—but the municipality of Berlin refused him
permission to cross the town in that array.

The circus formed a little independent universe with its
firemen, its police, and its maintenance staff of all kinds.
Everything about it was designed to dazzle, the brass, the
nickel, the glittering costumes, the blinding lights. We
passed enchanted hours there.

On the last day a dinner for sixty was given in the ring
itself for us and the press of Berlin. The orchestra under the
vast roof moderated its tones. From behind the scenes a
trumpeting or a roar occasionally rolled out to us. The artists waited on us. The serpent-man, with a supple contor-
tion, handed a dish across the table, jovial clowns poured out
the drinks, the juggler dropped a pile of plates, the con-
juror spared us his rabbits, Arabs, Redskins and Chinese bus-
tled about. The healthy smell of a well-kept circus in no
way spoilt our appetites.

Sarrasani never came to Paris and met a very sad end.
Two years later, under the reign of Hitler, he was ordered
to get rid of the Yugoslavs, the Israelites and the coloured
people whom he employed. "Sarrasani is master in his own
house," he replied haughtily, and rather than submit to
despotism, he resolved to leave with his whole circus for
South America. At Antwerp, where he was to embark, the

great tent which sheltered his elephants took fire and most of them perished. This was only the beginning of a series of misfortunes. In America the enterprise went bankrupt and Sarrasani died soon after, no doubt from grief.

## XIX

IT IS DIFFICULT for me to speak of Colette's friendships and more difficult to keep silent about them. How can I speak of them without assigning them an order of preference in Colette's heart, and at once admitting that I never questioned her about it? There is a risk, too, of letting my own feelings come into it in a way they should not. On the other hand, this book is made up of brief notes which do not pretend to exhaust anything, and whose value as sketches I wish to keep. I use whatever my memory supplies from day to day without forcing it in any way. There will therefore be many among Colette's friends who are absent and they must not be surprised at this.

All things considered it seems to me that the great friend of Colette was Marguerite Moréno. Their friendship was of much longer standing than any other, dating from the arrival of Colette in Paris. Marguerite, as is known, was the wife of the writer Marcel Schwob. The couple immediately adopted Colette and she was happy with them. Marcel Schwob, who knew everything, took to the little wild creature who knew nothing, and he seems to have guessed her worth. Colette did not so easily get acclimatized to Paris, to the dark Rue Jacob, to the artificiality of her new life and to a bohemianism for which she had no taste. In her dark hours she found a refuge with the Schwobs. For hours at a time Marcel Schwob used to tell her stories and read to her, translating English for her as he went along. Some spontaneous affectionate letters from Colette to Schwob still exist. Marcel Schwob died young.

For fifty years the two women friends kept losing sight of each other and finding each other again. In the early years of my relations with Colette they saw a great deal of each other. Marguerite Moréno, who had played tragedy and high comedy at the Comédie Française, had reached a difficult moment in her career. In spite of her talent she had no work.

"I assure you," Colette kept saying to her, "that you have a future as a comic actress. You ought to try, Marguerite."

"I shall never dare, my Colette," answered Marguerite, dropping her eyes, for she thought she had been born to speak verse.

When she did dare, it was a triumph, as we all know. She owed it to Colette who, it is true, owed a husband to her: it is not for me to say if this exchange was a good and friendly service.

I was often present when Colette and Moréno met. The contrast between them was great. Marguerite's knowledge was wide, her intelligence vast, her instinct less sure. She never made a gesture: with her expressionless face, her slow and level voice, she would relate irresistible stories bringing out their points with unequalled art. Colette on the other hand gave way to her laughter and enthusiasm, and abandoned herself entirely to the moment.

Friendship, like love, naturally speaks its true language only in a duet. I cannot therefore say to what extent Colette and Moréno confided in each other, but I think no other friend of Colette's unbosomed herself more. The other feminine friendships which I knew Colette to have, because of a difference in age and authority, and because of Colette's nature, brought out in her a more protective attitude. To oblige and serve a friend—sometimes even an unknown friend—Colette spared herself neither trouble nor action.

Hélène Picard and Colette had known each other since 1921. Colette had engaged Hélène as a secretary at *Le Matin* at the time when she was the literary director of it. Just as she spoke of Marguerite Moréno in *Le Fanal Bleu,* so Colette talked much of Hélène Picard in *L'Etoile Vesper.* Colette considered her a great poet. However friendly they were there remained something ceremonious about their relations. Towards Hélène Picard Colette combined a protective attitude with a certain respect, for she set poetry above prose, rather as she set the cat above the dog: "You know very well," she wrote to her, "that although I do not show it to you, I love you tenderly, with a carefully concealed respect for your genius and the great virtues of your solitude." Hélène Picard on her side never addressed Colette familiarly but worshipped her and kept the least thing she wrote. She imitated Colette's way of doing her hair and she must have been beautiful. I saw little of her and had difficulty in making her out. She was attacked very early by a strange disease of the bones, which prevented her from leaving her house, so that it was Colette who went to see her. She lived in Grenelle in a room high up where she had made for herself, with the aid of seraphic pictures, opalines and parakeets, all of the same blue, an ethereal little universe into which I never penetrated.

Colette had transferred to Germaine Beaumont the friendship which had bound her to the latter's mother, the writer Annie de Pène. Like Hélène Picard, Germaine Beaumont assisted Colette at *Le Matin* and shared her holidays at Rozven. Although they continued to be very fond of each other, as the letters they exchanged bear witness, they saw little of each other afterwards. Both being hard workers, they had no time. No doubt this was not the only motive for this slackening in their relations. Friendship is a sensitive thing. The man who suddenly appears in a woman's life, when her links of affection are already solidly formed, can easily appear an intruder. Whatever he may do, he encroaches on what others thought belonged to them, and gets in the way not of their faithfulness, but of their expressions of it. But does not the mere fact of breathing make it inevitable that you should injure someone? Let me add that the greater number of Colette's old friends eventually gave me support which I was never surprised had not been spontaneous.

Among these I shall quote Natalie Clifford Barney, an American of Paris, who, in the time of Monsieur Willy and Renée Vivien, held a literary salon in the Rue Jacob, in the former pavilion of Adrienne Lecouvreur. It was to her that Rémy de Gourmont addressed his *Lettres à l'Amazone*. She wrote, and writes still with an alert and caustic pen. Colette used to say of her: "She's a grand sort," and the praise was not negligible. Her friend the Duchesse de Clermont-Ton-

nerre, a great lady whose ambition was always to mingle
with the people, but who never did mingle with them, des-
perately shortsighted, tall and blond, was endowed with genuine originality and a real talent as a writer of memoirs. She
signed herself Elizabeth de Gramont, her maiden name.
Miss Barney and she used to come together to see Colette
and conjure up the memory of far off days.

Francis Carco, with his lock of hair, his pale complexion,
his cigarette and his heavy chin, cultivating a rose among
thorns, tenderness under cover of raillery, and friendship
above all things, gave me a friendly welcome from the first
day. Colette and I relied on him sometimes to take us out
of ourselves, in the days of the old Bals Musette and of the
Java houses of prostitution.* We dragged ourselves from the
Rue Sainte-Apolline to the Rue de Lappe and the Rue de
la Gaîté, finding routine where we were looking for vice.
Disapproval gave place to pity and the tour of the night life
circuit ended in a sentimental journey.

Among the more recent friends I distinguish two groups,
one which met at Saint-Tropez and the other connected
with the salon of the Princesse Edmond de Polignac. This
lady, born Singer, possessed an overwhelming fortune which
had come down to her from the sewing machine industry.
She lived in a great sad house at the angle of the Avenue
Henri-Martin and the Rue Cortambert, the whole of the
first floor of which was used for entertaining, the greater part
of it being taken up by a music room so vast that the two
Steinway concert pianos looked lost on their platform. A
good painter, an excellent musician, she saw to it that all

---

* There were in those days popular houses of this sort where respectable
people went to spend the evening, watching and chattering with the naked
girls when they were not "on duty."

that was worthwhile in music during the last fifty years was heard in her house, divining and encouraging budding talents and giving their first hearing to a quantity of works which afterwards made their way in the world. Lovers of music and society people, who were not always different people, met in her house. Cold in appearance, timid and intimidating with her blue glance, her jutting chin, her thin lips, the Princess always looked rather like a guest in her own house. She timidly gave enormous gifts to charitable works and founded institutions endowed with astronomical sums. She died quietly in England during the war.

Colette had adopted her because she looked like a multi-millionaire orphan, and because of the lucid humour with which she privately regarded herself. The Princess would climb up to Colette's flat when invited to mulled wine or to a cheese orgy, as though she were going to a feast. She was enchanted to find there a rusticity for which she longed, or so she thought:

"My dear," she would say to Colette, "I have no luck. I buy a little hut in the country, tell my architect to add a tiny little wing to it while I am in Venice. I return and what do I find? The Louvre," a word which, with her American accent through clenched teeth, because the "Louolouvre."

At the house of the Princesse de Polignac we met the Comtesse de Noailles and her sister the Princesse Hélène de Chimay. The two sisters also were sometimes allowed to come to mulled wine whose praise they subsequently spread throughout the town, proclaiming that they had discovered ambrosia. All it was, heated to the right temperature, was a bottle of Beaujolais to which had been added cinnamon, lemon and sugar.

Like all holidays groups, that of Saint-Tropez broke up in the autumn, but we went on seeing a good deal of some of its members in Paris, particularly Luc-Albert Moreau and Hélène Jourdan-Morhange. It was they who attracted us to the Forest of Rambouillet. As far as I was concerned this only meant returning there, for as a child I used to go with my family to see my mother's first cousin, the poet Gustave Kahn, who shared with Jules Laforgue the credit of having founded the symbolist school, and who owned a house adjoining the cloister at Montfort-L'Amaury.

Luc-Albert Moreau and Hélène Jourdan-Morhange had at Les Mesnuls, quite close to Montfort, a property composed of a garden and two little buildings. One of these was merely a garage with a living room above it, but under the thatched roof of the other there were three pleasantly proportioned ground-floor rooms. For years, winter and summer, we went there to lunch on Sunday, in accordance with unalterable rites. Cat and dog took part in the fun, incidentally always knowing without having to be told that it was Sunday and we were all going out.

After we had all got into the car, the first stop was at a cheese shop in the Place de la Madeleine. Colette got out. The shopkeeper was ready waiting for her, with cheeses which fortunately were not too firm, having been ripened especially for this exceptional connoisseur. The discussion took a long time, and to me it was tiresomely technical. The final upshot was three or four cheeses, half melting into each other, which soon turned the car into a stink-pot, but whose savour was so superior as to have only the most fleeting connection with what we normally call a cheese.

There was a second stop in the Avenue Victor Hugo, at

a shop of a butcher who had been selected out of a thousand for his good meat and also, I think, for the bantering look with which he welcomed his client, an everlasting cigarette butt stuck in the corner of his mouth. When Colette rushed in a contest began between those two people equally endowed with a ready tongue, although for different purposes. The problem was not only to obtain from this butcher steaks of superlative quality, but also a tribute of cheap bits destined for the stray cats of Les Mesnuls. At last we left Paris behind. Forty miles away, Luc-Albert Moreau was already cherishing the wood embers which were to receive this provender.

Colette's name for him was "Village saint" and she describes him thus: ". . . shining eyes and ruddy complexion the colour of a winter apple, the complexion of a man who likes to live in the open air and drink wine. It seemed right that he should be short and rather stocky, unusually nimble and quick, with a timid and sometimes abrupt way of speaking. When he stays quiet he withdraws into himself, sunk as though in prayer, with his eyes down and an indolent expression, his whole person stamped with a deceptive gentleness."

Hélène Jourdan-Morhange, short, with blue eyes and the look of a round-headed cherub, was commonly considered by all musicians to be a great violinist, but her career had been interrupted by persistent neuritis. She was a devotee of Ravel, on whom she wrote a book called *Ravel et Nous,* with a preface by Colette. And she worshipped Colette, whom she came to see almost every day.

Nothing seems easier than to grill *entrecôte minute* on wood embers, but it took no less than the combined efforts

of Colette and Luc-Albert Moreau, both of them in a state
of grace, to bring it off to perfection. There is the quality
of the fire, the position of the griller, the right moment for
turning the steaks with a fork resembling a devil's strident,
adding salt and pepper, and serving them crowned with a
lump of butter.

In the same way, once a year at home, we had truffle-day.
But that could only take place if the bank-account allowed,
for Colette used to say: "If I can't have too many truffles,
I'll do without truffles," and she declared they should be
eaten like potatoes. We waited until, with the coming of the
frost, Périgord should send the finest of its mushrooms. It
appears that cleaning them is an art and Colette would not
entrust the responsibility for this to anyone else. Then you
put half a bottle of dry champagne in a black stew-pan, with
some bits of bacon fat lightly browned, salt and pepper.
When this mixture boils you throw in the truffles. A divine
and slightly suspect odour, like everything that smells really
good, floats through the house. Under no pretext must the
truffles leave the stew-pan; the scented sauce is served sep-
arately, hot in port glasses, and anyone who does not declare
himself ready to leave Paradise or Hell for such a treat is
not worthy to be born again.

Matter, perhaps, but what a spirit this matter has! Pro-
gressing thus from being exacting to harsh in one's choice,
one reaches a point where one wants nothing but the fittest
word, the very marrow of things, their essence, their perfume.

What a lot of people came to Les Mesnuls, almost all of
whom were friends of ours too, or became so. I should never

end if I were to set down the whole list of them, so I will name a few at random: the musicians Ravel, Auric, Poulenc, the painters Segonzac, Dignimont, Daragnès, the professors Mondor and Pasteur Vallery-Radot, the architect Jean-Charles Moreux, Claude-Roger Marx, Julien Cain. . . . When I remember the ten years preceding the war and think of the varied activities of Colette—collaborations of all kinds, occasional work, lectures, the film, the radio—I am surprised that we were able to go out every evening either to the theatre or to see friends belonging to all worlds. Celebrity gradually caught Colette in its toils. One receives it at first without distrust, and when one wants to curb it it is too late. Very soon there was no longer an investigation in which Colette was not invited to take part, no jury on which she was not invited to sit. A hundred projects were submitted to her, her post began to grow out of all measure, strangers, professional or just idle, knocked at her door, the pile of books and photographs to be autographed grew higher. With what robust good humour did she face this tide!

Later, with the arrival of age and fatigue and physical ills, I had necessarily to filter these visitors of Colette's. Anyone who has fulfilled that task, of erecting a screen between a celebrated person and the hoards of those who wish to approach, knows how easy it is to acquire an unpopularity from which one cannot hope to recover.

The first result of this encroaching renown was to make Saint-Tropez uninhabitable for Colette. The peaceful village of our first years, devoted to fishing and pottering, had turned into a hive of tourists. On the wharves, a double row of cars hid the view of the port. The yachts had chased away the old boats, the bars had become dance-halls where every imaginable kind of couple stayed on until the first light. The few hundred yards which separated "La Treille Muscate" from the village hardly protected us. A visit to Colette formed part of every holiday programme. Even the morning swim had henceforth its spectators, many of whom came by sea. One of these navigators called out one day as he landed on our little shore covered with seaweed: "But it's Arcadia!" We didn't ask so much of it as that.

Our little property had the flimsiest of enclosures, a wooden fence giving on to the coast-path and an iron one on to the road. Both of them had locks, perhaps, but if we used them we should have to bother with keys. How could we decide to do that when, for example, one of the tele-graph poles, for greater convenience, was planted in the middle of our garden? The men who mended the wires, which were often upset by the mistral, had free access to our property. However one of them, standing outside the fence, one day asked me for permission to enter. Astonished at such precaution I raised my eyes to a splendid specimen of humanity, a veritable block of granite. Stripped to the waist, he revealed a vast carcass with powerful shoulders and chest muscles.

"Why of course you can come in," I said to him.

Five minutes later he had not budged.

"But why don't you come in?"

"It's because of the dog," he said lowering his eyes.

I noticed then that the bulldog Souci was close beside me. One of the smallest specimens of her race who had neither any desire to bite nor any teeth to do it with.

"What do you mean, the dog?" I asked.

Without the least shame, the man let fall from the height of his six feet these simple words:

"I'm afeared of them."

Ah, the South!

Colette decided to sell. Whether it was a question of selling or buying, once she had decided, these operations brooked no delay. The first purchaser was the right one, the seller's price had to be accepted on the spot for fear he should change his mind. More patient than anyone in her work, in any other matter procrastination was intolerable to her. She preferred to make mistakes and keep her mind free. So decided in her tastes and wishes, the indecision of others always left her astonished.

"Are you hungry?" she would ask me before a meal.

"I really don't know."

She raised her arms to heaven.

"How can one not even know whether one is hungry or not!"

It must be admitted that, with her, hunger was something incredibly imperious. If by chance she had to wait, her face took on a tragic expression. She would begin to growl like an animal, largely out of fun, of course, but this fun helped her to keep a hold on herself. How powerful was the animal instinct in her and how praiseworthy her control of it! She could readily have given way to anger if she had not at the same time been so reasonable. "I've forbidden myself a righteous anger once again," she would say to me, "but how it hurts!"

The first purchaser in this case was the actor Charles Vanel. He got the house with everything in it for the price he wanted to pay for it. He sold it soon after he had acquired it.

"How nice it is not to have the responsibility of owning a house and having caretakers," repeated Colette, "I won't have another." A heavy wistaria, stretching all along the eighty yards of an enclosing wall, decided otherwise one Sunday when, returning from Les Mesnuls by an unusual route, we passed through Méré, a suburb of Montfort-l'Amaury. The property, which was for sale, comprised a little house without style or grace, in front of which there spread a cedar with powerful branches, a big kitchen garden, and a beautiful garden almost deserving the ambitious name of park, which had been given to it. The property presented, among other inconveniences, a couple of bad-tempered caretakers relentlessly installed in the outbuildings, cultivating the kitchen garden, supposedly on the *métayage* system, and quite obviously determined to carry on a silent war with their masters, whoever they might be. But the wistaria carried the day, and that very evening I went to see its owner, with instructions to accept his price if he condescended to mention one, and on no account to bargain with him. Although such procedure momentarily aroused his suspicion and made him wonder whether we had not got wind of a treasure that the house concealed, I got my way.

The property was called "Le Parc" and we did not feel we ought to change a name so full of mystery and novelty. The blue cedar, growing close to the house, made it dark, sad and damp. We had to choose between it and the sun. Colette did not hesitate: the tree which was the pride of the "Parc" was cut down and finished as logs in the chimney. The caretakers caused us all those annoyances that their cast of mind and body promised. It was at Méré that the exodus in June 1940 surprised us.

# XX

COLLECTING OUR personal possessions from "La Treille Muscate," and installing ourselves in the Palais Royal and at Méré, made a good many removals in the same year, which Colette briskly organised. The month of August 1939 found us for the first time undecided as to where we should go for our holidays. Our friends the Léopold Marchands persuaded us to spend them with them at Dieppe. With its cool climate, pale light and grey sea, the contrast with our meridional hours was complete. Dieppe, with its old-fashioned air, its conventional seaside, and its villas, some of which date from the reign of Charles X, did not lack charm. The Duchesse de Berry, Madame Récamier, the English of the Victorian age, with their blond young ladies in crinolines and the bohemians of Bloomsbury, still haunted it a little. The Hôtel Métropole, which has now disappeared, turned out to be excellent: grey shrimps, unknown in the South, were eaten there by the bushel.

Our holiday cheerfulness did not make us entirely deaf to the war which was approaching. Like the whole of Europe, we had lived for two years in a climate heavy with threats, one result being that one no longer entirely believed in them, and the other that it deadened any deep sense of revolt: "Oh, well, it can't be helped!" one ended by saying.

Léopold Marchand was called up in the last days of August and left in a hurry, accompanied by his wife. Colette and I remained in a town which was gradually emptying. But the weather was beautiful, and if the men of my age-group were not mobilised, nothing recalled us to Paris, so we decided, war or no war, to spend the greater part of the month of September at Dieppe.

At the end of a very few days, a sort of silence established itself between us. We could not detach our thoughts from Paris, we imagined its stupor, its anguish, its homes whose men had gone.

"What are you thinking of?" I said abruptly to Colette.

It took exceptional circumstances to make me put this question, which was taboo between us.

"Of the same thing as you," she answered.

"Very well then, we'll leave to-morrow morning."

If it had not been for the terrible news from Poland, the war at first would hardly have seemed a serious matter. There was the distribution of gas masks which was rather like a play. One man got suffocated in trying his on, but he was happily the only victim during this conflict.

The first air-raid warning occurred two or three days after the declaration of war. With the help of a great to-do about "civic duty," "setting an example" and so on, I persuaded Colette to go down to the cellar. We had an aged concierge, prematurely worn out by a lustfulness thanks to which she had recently driven her husband into his grave, and deaf into the bargain. By all joining forces, we tenants of the house succeeded where the sirens had failed, and she awoke from her sleep and immediately began to yell "The defeat is upon us! The Prussians are here!" After which she followed us.

We spent a few sad hours in a dark and evil-smelling cellar. When we were released, we found our wonderful concierge had left the keys of the entrance-gate in her lodge. We had to find a ladder and break a window. We waited exhausted in the dim early-morning light. Thenceforward nothing could persuade Colette to go down into the shelters, even at the height of the bombardments of 1944.

Colette did not wait for an instant before laying in provisions. When troubles arise this is the first act of the French country people. They have seen so many wars and invasions, the ebb and flow of so many armies! They do not even need to know history. Pauline, who comes from the Limousine, has in her blood the memory of the robber barons, of the League, the Fronde and the Revolution. In the heart of the provinces insults remain whose origin no one can remember. When Pauline complained of the Cat, in spite of her perfections, she called her "Marie-Antoinette," although she was ignorant no doubt of the Affair of the Necklace and the degree of unpopularity which that brought upon the poor queen. In Gascony, the supreme insult remains "English swine," but those who use it do not know that it still alludes to the English who occupied Guyenne in the Hundred Years' War. I heard it in 1942, at a time when everyone in the Tarn was listening to the English radio and praying for our allies.

Throughout the whole war, Colette showed herself to be an incomparable quartermaster. A grasshopper in other respects, she was an ant where provender was concerned. As early as this first September, she filled the cellar with coal right up to the top. She organised a system of parcels from all the friends we had outside Paris, in particular with two women-farmers in the neighbourhood of Nantes, who for love of the fields, had formerly left their families, accomplished the work of three men, possessed a model she-wolf which they passed off as their dog, and wrote enchanting letters. These kitchen-garden transactions necessitated a correspondence of ministerial proportions.

Was France preparing her armies as strenuously as could be desired? At any rate she was neglecting nothing in the way of propaganda. The words "information" and "propaganda" unfortunately began at that time, both here and elsewhere, to be used as though they were synonymous, and the world still seems not to have recovered from the confusion.

The appointment of Jean Giraudoux as Minister of Information puzzled Colette. "Curious," she said to me, "there's a writer who most of the time proceeds by negation, defining things and people by what they are not: 'He was neither this . . . nor that . . . nor the other . . .' and he's the man they choose to inform us!"

Colette and I soon found ourselves taken on by Paris-Mondial. This radio station was used for transmitting to overseas countries. Because of the time differences the programs took place at most unusual hours. For us it was three in the morning. Colette spoke to American students. Afterwards the station played them French plays, which I presented in a brief talk . . . in English. I did this boldly since I had the definite impression that the Paris-Mondial station was not very powerful and that my near-English got lost somewhere in the ether. I am very much afraid that the same thing happened with Colette's talks. She wrote them out, spoke two or three lines in French, and an American woman-speaker read the rest, translating as she went along. Anyone other than Colette would have thought that, in these conditions, she could take less trouble with her texts, but she did not have two ways of writing. One will be able to judge by the only one of these talks which has been recovered and which figures under the title of *"La Chaufferette"* in *Journal à Rebours*. I have not given up all hope of finding one or two others.

At this very moment some letters addressed by Colette to a woman friend, Mademoiselle Bénard-Fleury, have been brought to me so that I can copy them. Almost immediately my eyes fall on the following passage:

"We are broadcasting. I speak to America through an interpreter on the nights of Sunday to Monday at 2:30 A.M. But since I wait for my husband who speaks—in English—at 3:20, it means we don't get to bed till quarter past four. Apart from that . . ."

Even in quite a faithful memory fifteen years blur certain details: mine had retained neither the day nor the exact hours of our broadcasts. I only remember certain November nights, when a thick fog added to the blackout of Paris. Our little car pierced the gloom as it groped its way to the Rue de Grenelle. In the courtyard of the post office we bumped into the shadows of telegraph boys and ghostly motor-bikes. Inside the building, which was brilliantly lit, the hours of waiting dragged on, with that vague hollow in the stomach which a persistent desire to sleep gives one. Happily there was a canteen where technicians, maintenance-men, and artists mingled; Colette loved that atmosphere of a team, happy to pull her weight with the others and in no way claiming a special place for herself. Her niceness towards ordinary people came from the fact that she did not consider them as such.

*Bella-Vista*, which appeared in 1937, is the first of her volumes of stories, and was followed by *Chambre d'Hôtel*, *Le Képi* and *Gigi*. This form, which thenceforth she preferred, was not the sign of any impoverishment in her, nor of less patience, but of a desire for greater brevity. More and more she refused whatever was easy for her, descriptions of the country among other things. There are none to be found in *Gribiche* or in *Gigi*.

"Hello!" I would say to her. "Have you torn up what you wrote yesterday?"

"Yes, I found I was writing Colette."

Nothing is more unfaltering than the writing of those stories, or happier than their touch. The Goya-like figure of the matron in *Gribiche*, the end of *Rendez-Vous*, which conjures up in a few modest phrases the whole solidarity between man and man, the central scene of *Le Képi*, the apparition of the mother, lamp in hand in *Le Tendron*, the confession of *La Dame du Photographe*, are things that cannot be forgotten.

*Chambre d'Hôtel* was to have been called *Gîte de Hasard*, but Colette allowed herself to be influenced by Francis Carco. It is a good title for Carco, but less good for Colette. She subsequently regretted this over-precise title and its provocative air, but it was too late.

After so much labour and the nights at Paris-Mondial, Colette was at the end of her tether by the close of winter, and had bronchitis into the bargain. I persuaded her to go and rest for a few days at Nice, without me but accompanied by Hélène Jourdan-Morhange. One evening, when she was coming back with Hélène from the cinema, a man brushed past her on the Promenade des Anglais, snatched her hand-bag which contained three thousand francs, and made off at top speed. Colette immediately reported the matter to the chief of police, in the hope of getting back not her three thousand francs, but the bag and her papers. They were indeed found and returned, since the first anxiety of robbers of this kind is to get rid of anything that might lead to their discovery. The local papers mentioned the assault and the name of the victim.

Two days later Colette received a note with these simple words in an untutored hand-writing: "I didn't know it was you." The envelope contained three thousand francs. But Colette had declared a round figure and remembered afterwards that one of the thousand franc notes had been broken into, so that this charming and delicate robber was out of pocket by it. The story was so much talked about that a Paris newspaper declared Madame Colette certainly had a great deal of imagination and knew better than anyone how to take care of her own publicity.

Within an interval of three months of each other, first the Cat and then the dog reached the end of their lives and received that merciful death which is too often refused to humans. We had had them thirteen years. When Colette worked in the afternoons the Cat used to sleep against her side. She would wake from time to time, pull Colette by the sleeve, give her a long look of love and ecstasy, and fall asleep again.

In the expression of her grief, Colette was restrained as always. She was merely silent for a few days. But many years later, I would hear her sigh sometimes: "Oh, that Cat!"

She never had any more animals and people have been astonished at this. But the Cat proved to be irreplaceable: some animals can have a sufficiently strong personality to impose an emptiness after them. A dog, yes, with its widespread goodwill, its unvarying tenderness—another dog would have been possible. But already Colette was walking less well, and fearing that she would no longer be able to give them enough exercise, she gave up animals.

# XXI

THAT DORMANT, unreal war turned from one day to the next into a genuine and terrible war. Then came the breach suddenly opened, Dunkirk, the honourable blindness which left us confident. . . . At the beginning of June I installed Colette at Méré pending other holiday plans. I myself went every day to Paris to provide *Marie-Claire* and *Match* with a not very effective literary direction, and returned every evening to Méré. On June 11, after I had crossed the Bois de Boulogne and was entering Paris, I thought the streets had an unaccustomed air, both sad and feverish. People were loading cars and stowing luggage, smoke rose here and there, coming from the archives which the ministries were burning. At *Paris-Soir* they were moving and part of the services was already en route for Clermont-Ferrand. As soon as I had made a few arrangements with my bank and elsewhere, I returned to Méré earlier than usual by roads which from hour to hour were becoming more and more congested. I told Colette what was happening and suggested that we should leave, but she refused. It was no good pointing out to her that Méré might from one moment to another be turned into a battlefield, and that we should not be able to stay on there even if we wanted to; she remained firm. Méré was so calm!

"All right then, never mind," I said without insisting. "Let's go for a little drive."

I took Colette along the roads which I had just left and she became solemn. The roads had that air which she described later on when she spoke of "France slithering on her own surface."

"We passed ox-carts, forage-wagons, huge cars thick with dust, wheelbarrows and charabancs. . . . Those fields of ripe grass where every hollow was filled with groups of people asleep, with cars caparisoned with mattresses, with sleeping children rolled in bath wraps, a pair of doves in a cage, a fox-terrier tied to a tree, a young girl huddling in a man's overcoat. . . ."

Colette resigned herself. Thinking that it was reasonable for us to follow the means whereby we lived, in other words the newspapers, I suggested taking her first to the Corrèze, where her daughter lived.

"And when do we leave?"

"Very soon. At four in the morning."

She looked at me and saw that I was right. At the hour agreed we left, weighed down with luggage and tins of gasoline, Pauline in the back. The roads were crowded with cars of every kind. Tremendous bottlenecks occurred here and there and while they lasted there was nothing to do but wait gloomily. "Ah," said Pauline with a sigh during one of these waits, "we ought never to have let *them* get in." It was logic itself.

It took us barely six hours to reach the Loire, which was

very little in view of the fact that some cars, which left several hours later than we, took the whole day. After the Loire, all went well and we arrived at Curemonte towards five in the evening.

Colette de Jouvenel lived in a fantastic place. On a sort of wedge-like eminence stood two medieval castles, lofty and narrow, barely ten yards apart, whose history was obscure. They were threatened not with ruin, as this had already occurred, but with complete collapse: stones and beams rained down from time to time. But the outhouses, running the length of the enclosing wall, restored, arranged and furnished with taste, made a comfortable dwelling. Colette de Jouvenel offered us hospitality there. It was a gracious haven in the storm.

If I have not yet spoken of Colette de Jouvenel and her relations with her mother, and if I say little of her now, it is not from lack of interest or sympathy, far from it. But I am striving to write here only of what I know well. I admire those biographers who, in their appreciation of the character and motives of their subjects, never hesitate. I feel much less assured.

What seems certain is that, as long as her daughter was very young, Colette showed herself the most attentive and experienced of mothers. But though she did not thrust her child away from her from one day to the next, with the severity of female animals, she thought that after a certain age "succeeding generations are not made to live together." She also thought that, if she kept her daughter with her, she would have to choose between her work and her. My entry into the life of Colette had no effect on this arrangement. If the little Colette, who was then thirteen years old and at boarding school, thought otherwise at that time, it would not have surprised me. How can children who see one or other of their parents forming new links not feel themselves in danger of receiving a less constant affection? Yet not to divorce is no better a solution to this painful problem, for discord between parents upsets their children just as much.

Every time I saw Colette and her daughter together, they were experiencing the greatest pleasure at being with each other, but where feelings are concerned they both had great shyness, which does not encourage demonstrations and risks confusing reserve with coldness and discretion with lack of trust. When, for no particular reason, they remained for long months without seeing each other, they regretted it equally. On meeting again they sought for a contact which was never quite established. Happily the years only improved these relations, and at the end mother and daughter came together again.

A strange existence now began. The weather was fine and that walled enclosure, our refuge, was brilliant with flowers. The two phantom castles reared their carcasses, pierced again and again by swallows; from the half-deserted village which they dominated, no sound arose. We organised a life like shipwrecked people, sharing the different tasks: I myself, armed with a compass-saw, a boarding-axe and even with a scythe . . . At that time when everything was falling to pieces around us, we enjoyed such silence and solitude as we had not known for a long time. But that peace was like certain dreams which do not altogether deceive us, since we feel through our sleep that a nightmare is near. The nightmare came to us through the ether. Each time that we turned on the radio, an army in defeat broke over us, a state in de-cay. Our quiet life seemed culpable to us and anguish seized us in the midst of our well-being. Right up to the day when that quavering voice arose which gave hope to some but already chilled the rest with the darkest of forebodings. . . .

Colette had immediately set to work again. That task of writing, of which she had so long wanted to rid herself, had become for her, to put it at its lowest, a habit, something automatic. Clear-sighted about herself, she was the first to recognise it. It was at Curemonte that she wrote: "No matter how ingrained our job is, nor for how long we have done it, it leaves us when an honour, a disaster or an exodus, involving a whole nation, sweeps us up in their ground swells. . . . But at the end of a long road it comes back; I did not foresee that I should travel so far to come up against a table—boundary, obstacle, reef; on legs like stilts, low enough for a bed table, or wobbly as the pedestal table of a hotel—against a writing-table. Every sight I see provokes me to the same duty, which is perhaps merely a temptation: to write, to depict."

In short, in the last period of her life she wrote for writing's sake, without any idea of publication. Freed from the labour of creating characters and bringing a plot to a head, she gave herself up, alone with her high standards, to a touching struggle with form. The themes are few, taken up twenty or a hundred times. The writing, firm to begin with, little by little reveals her fatigue until at last it rejoins that of Sido's last letter, to which she refers on the last page of *La Naissance du Jour*, Sido who had given birth to her and whom she has recreated, Sido to whom when she was dying she stretched out her arms, to her and to the enchanted gardens of her childhood.

Yes, life at Curemonte was sweet. In the village, an amiable woman, Madame Vayssier, ran with much vigour a little inn on which the increasing restrictions did not weigh too heavily, and when we desired it she cooked excellently for us. Curemonte lies on a steep slope. Colette de Jouvenel's two dogs, a little dachshund, active as a ferret, and a fat and amiable boxer-bitch, had immediately marked me down as a lover of walks and used to wait for me at the gate even before I myself knew that I wanted to go out. Colette sometimes accompanied us. A sharp descent brought us to the banks of the Sourdoise, a little river running between willows. But the climb up was steep and Colette would stop, complaining of her hip. How insidious is this disease of arthritis! Without it Colette would still for a long time have been almost indefatigable. From year to year it reduced her movement without ever letting up, until it had pinned her down like a bird caught in oil.

Comfortable though our existence was at Curemonte, before three weeks had passed Colette was longing to get back to Paris. That was where the drama was taking place and it was to that that she felt drawn. She wanted to watch the reflection of it on human faces and to feel herself one with them. "I'm used to spending my wars in Paris," she said. I felt as she did that when the rest of the world is undergoing torment, security is an air which quickly becomes poisoned, and I suggested to her that we should go to Lyons, and there prepare our return journey.

At Lyons we found the offices of our newspapers and

many familiar faces. Installed in a vast hotel-room with a view on the Rhône, Colette had nothing to complain about except not being in Paris. She even formed a friendship there . . . with some mice, who were busy in the room. She put crumbs of bread for them at the hole where they came out.

"Do you mind leaving those crumbs," she said one day to the manservant, with his brush, "they're for the mice." "I can do better than that," he answered, going out and coming back with traps. He expected compliments, but got roundly abused and retired without understanding.

Once again Colette began to work. At Lyons she finished the unpublished part of *Journal à Rebours*.

To get gasoline for our return to Paris was not so easy, and took a lot of arranging. We saw the Prefect, we visited the Mayor and President Herriot. Separated by their different works, Herriot and Colette always looked, whenever they met, like two college chums finding each other again. The President has always made not only flattering but affectionate remarks about Colette, and at her death he dedicated to her an article that I am not likely to forget.

I am sure that he would not object to my revealing an unexpected correspondence which took place between them at the time when Colette was living on the mezzanine floor at 9 Rue de Beaujolais, during the period of her first stay in the Palais-Royal. In front of her windows there stood at that time, in the garden itself, a café called "La Rotonde," where chess-players used to meet. By way of another particularity— I do not say attraction—it had no sewage-system, so that the famous carts of the Richier Company, which all old Parisians remember, came once a month to remove the sewage, causing a horrible smell which penetrated into all the neighbouring flats. Colette complained about it to the Beaux-Arts which, ironically enough, was the Ministry concerned and of which Herriot was then Minister. There was a letter from Colette which, although written in much more veiled terms than the celebrated scatological letter of the Princesse Palatine, did not for all that lack savour, if I may so put it. Herriot replied very aptly:

Dear Friend,
        This is clearly a matter to be treated in the innermost closets of the Ministry. . . .

It was "La Rotonde" which was suppressed.

Lyons is a beautiful town which does not deserve the austere reputation it has been given. My first stay there had been in 1915 in the barracks of the Foreign Legion, to which I belonged, when I was convalescing from a wound.

We left for Paris in the first ten days of August. When we reached the control post of the occupied zone, a German, wearing a benevolent smile, examined me with attention and found nothing suspicious about me. For Colette it was otherwise.

"You, Jewess," he said.

Colette's denials appeared to leave him unconvinced. Next he examined Pauline. With her very black hair, since turned white, her big yellow eyes and unpolished complexion, Pauline represented at its purest what we call the Saracen type, without any very precise idea what we mean by that.

"You, *certainly* Jewess," insisted the German.

I don't really know what took me then, what impulse to fly to the help of two women unjustly suspected, what ridiculous distaste for dissimulation, even towards the enemy, what stupid pride, what insane revolt against a ban which I thought odious.

"You're utterly mistaken," I said to the German in his own tongue, "I alone here am of Jewish birth."

He immediately went to refer the matter to a young rosy-faced officer, very neat and elegant who, with a grimace of supreme disgust, with both hands thrust far from his offended sight that car filled with the refuse of humanity, crying:

"*Zurück, zurück, wir brauchen keine Juden.*"

We were thus forced to return to Lyons, very crestfallen. Three weeks later we left again, armed with a letter of recommendation from the Swedish Consulate, which earned for us much consideration and clickings of heels. If they had examined us more closely they would have seen Colette had with her a little loaded revolver, which followed her everywhere, which she always kept on her work-table, and from which, in spite of my objurgations, she would not be parted. She had slipped it into a glove and, even while she was answering the Germans, she was airily swinging in front of her this empty glove, one finger of which, wonderful to relate, remained stiff and pointed.

During this journey the car for the first time broke down occasionally, so that night had fallen by the time we reached Paris. My nerves were on edge and I did not see a red light, but I heard a whistle. I was afraid lest the penalties for such offences had become extremely severe and I expected the worst. A rather stout policeman came to the door of the car and said in a gentle voice:

"Don't you stop at the red lights?"

"Yes, of course, but I didn't see it. We come from a distance and I'm tired."

"Oh! I see, you've come from a distance. That's why you perhaps don't know that . . . we've got visitors. So a word of advice . . . walk on tiptoe."

From the ironical tone and the look of connivance we got a good impression of the Parisian in occupied Paris.

# XXII

FOUR YEARS of little problems each day more difficult, of crafty courage shared with everyone. . . . To endure living on tenterhooks and imposing on oneself a relative lightheartedness became a duty. Waiting, waiting! . . .

The little revolver, object of so much care, fell a victim to strict regulations and went down the drain. But we had not finished with firearms. Much later, at the time when I was in the greatest danger and when assaults against the Germans took place every day, we found at the back of a hanging cupboard a sporting gun, forgotten and abandoned there by the previous tenant. If it had been found in the course of a search it would have meant the death penalty. Colette, Pauline and I held a council of war and decided on a nocturnal expedition in the course of which the awkward gun would be carelessly chucked into the Seine.

We left at nightfall, Colette and I walking in front, Pauline following, with the offensive object, carefully wrapped up, on her shoulder. It is surprising how like a gun a disguised gun still looks. We pretended to be a little group out for a walk, but we looked like a commando.

When we got to the Place du Théatre Français there was a sudden rush of people: the Germans were making a raid. I pressed Colette's arm, but she knew as well as I that we must not quicken our steps. Without turning round I threw over my shoulder to Pauline:

"Go on walking as calmly as possible, Pauline; and don't look as if you are trying to hide the gun."

"The gun?" said Pauline, "I got rid of it behind a doorway a long time ago."

Fortunately I never heard the end of the story. But I can imagine a concierge opening the door next morning, and a tradesman and passerby all drawing back with horror from the untouchable object. . . . I give this beginning of a scenario to anyone who would like it.

The car had been taken from us and communications in Paris were becoming difficult. Colette was following successive treatments, all equally useless, for her injured hip. A doctor recommended bicycling to her and she felt attracted by a therapy which would at least give her fresh air in the Bois de Boulogne. I seized the occasion to yield at last to a temptation which had teased me since my youth. At that time I thought there was nothing more enviable than a racing-bicycle, but the children of the middle-classes were brought up in parsimony, and such an expense was out of question. When I began to earn money, I went shares with a friend in buying a little second-hand car, a bargain which turned out to be chiefly a bargain for those who had to do the expensive repairs it needed: I had not means enough to acquire a bicycle as well. Now at last, at the age of fifty-two, I realised this long-cherished dream: I bought a little bicycle all aluminum, exquisite as a jewel and neat as a new pin and mounted on tubular tires. It had no mud-guard and when it rained I was spattered from head to foot. The saddle was very high, the handlebars very low, and I used to get an indescribable back-ache. But I was delighted; one should never hesitate to get back to one's youth.

Colette and I used to go to the Bois. Colette, although she was sixty-seven, pedalled easily, suffering much less than when she walked since she had not her weight to carry. I sped proudly before her on my winged steed, returning and circling round her like a hunting dog. When it came to indulging in childish ways she and I had always been the same age.

Colette, whose bed had successively occupied every corner of her flat, had finally chosen to put it right against the window. From then on she worked sitting up on her divan-bed, her back supported by cushions. She would stay like this for hours, and later for days, helped by a bodily suppleness which never abandoned her. From her window she watched the humble folk of Paris passing, wondering if they were sufficiently well fed, worrying about the children, noticing the increasing shabbiness of their clothes. "How do they manage?" she said to me. "Will they last out to the end? Oh dear! it worries me."

This worry is reflected in *De Ma Fenêtre* which appeared in 1942. This book is full of advice on how to feel less cold and to eat better. In the deepest part of her being she felt herself one with the hard working Parisian, struggling with the shortages. In the Palais-Royal she would go into the shops and question the children in the garden, forging in fact that link with the Palais-Royal which has never since been broken. Through their unfailing instinct the people of Paris were aware of that solicitude and that torment: it was they who throughout three days filed in silence before her door, they who lay upon her tomb touching, anonymous bouquets.

What with the incessant bombings of London and the increasing losses borne by English shipping, nothing came to cheer the dark days of 1941, until the moment when the astonishing news broke upon the world that Hitler was attacking Russia.

Just as Madame de Noailles could no longer keep silent, I could no longer restrain my natural optimism. I gave it free play.

"The war's over," I said to Colette.

"You're mad!"

"It may go on three or four years more, but for me, in the certainty of the absolute, Hitler has already disappeared and the German soldiers you see passing at this moment are no longer anything but ghosts."

These ghosts came to arrest me a few months later, on December 12, 1941. Pauline entered my room. Pauline only uses the third person every now and then, and it is the last thing that Colette and I would have demanded of her. She speaks her mind with princes and the great ones of this world, but she was so troubled that she addressed me in the following terms:

"Monsieur, it is the Germans who have come to arrest Monsieur."

I looked at my watch. It was twenty past seven.

"What a pity, Pauline," I answered, "I was sleeping so well."

But immediately I thought of Colette and my heart contracted. As far as I was concerned I had got used to the idea that I might be arrested one day. But I had never shared these fears with Colette and she was going to receive this shock without being prepared for it. I knew what she would feel and I was also sure that she would show nothing of it.

A German non-commissioned officer, helmeted and wearing round his neck the chain of the *Feldgendarmerie*, had followed Pauline and told me, politely I must say, what I was to take with me.

"Go and warn Madame," I said to Pauline.

I found Colette up, and as much mistress of herself as I hoped. She helped me to pack my bag. We only exchanged useful words. The *Feldwebel* waited. The other exit from the flat was guarded by an ordinary soldier, a fanatical little red-head, much more aggressive than his superior.

Colette accompanied me to the head of the staircase. We looked at each other. We were both smiling and we exchanged a quick kiss.

"Don't worry," I said. "All will be well."

"Off you go," she said to me with a friendly tap on my shoulder.

In the serious moments of our life in common we never acted otherwise, without having ever discussed or agreed about it. I am not in the least pretending to quote ourselves as an example. I can well understand that such a determination to dominate one's feelings might be called inhuman, and that one might urge the warmth and the help that emotions and alarm expressed on both sides can offer. But I am touching here on one of the essential traits of Colette's character without a knowledge of which her work, to my mind, is not entirely understandable. And if, in order to keep the secret of our most private understanding I were forced to give an uncertain image of her, I would rather wash my hands of the whole matter.

I well know that this stoicism and its outward show are what one expects least of Colette. But I know too that those who have dwelt on her work with an attention at all sustained, must have had a suspicion that her personality is more complex than they had first thought. . . . Free, uncurbed, given up to the moment—I have already had to contradict this widespread opinion several times here and to introduce the word severity where it seemed to have no place. What a lot of mistakes must thus have been made, unless it is thought that discipline, strictness with oneself, and the will-power needed for composition, may be put on and off like a disguise beside one's work table.

Ready to compromise, not very aggressive in the ordinary things of life, mistrustful of heroes, indulgent—almost to excess—to all weaknesses, Colette attained without effort the greatest possible firmness of soul. Absolutely feminine in her coquetry, her type of jealousy, a certain irrationalism, and also in her submission, no one could be more virile in adversity, and in sudden moments where greatness is involved.

But just as it needed a puff of wind to raise her hair so that one saw her forehead, only circumstances in which they were required drew from her those high virtues, which then became as natural to her as her familiar tone and manner were in ordinary circumstances.

It was just the same with her work. Her sentences always suited their purpose and that purpose most often was to paint ordinary humanity and the landscapes that you see everywhere. But if she had occasion to write about a circumstance or a man greater than the common measure, she at once surpassed herself and her tone took on an unparalleled amplitude and force. Read this passage which describes the uniform of Marcel Proust, receiving some friends in the hall of the Ritz Hotel, a Proust who was soon to die:

". . . An ordinary full-dress uniform, in short, but disarranged as though by a furious wind which, pushing his hat on to the nape of his neck, crumpling his linen and the restless ends of his tie, filling with black ash the furrows in his cheek, the hollows of his eye-sockets and his gasping mouth, was driving this tottering young man of fifty to the brink of the grave."

Colette claimed that a wild animal—and the cat is a wild animal—prudently avoids showing how far it can leap. If one day it finds it necessary to make a prodigious bound, would one deny that it had always had the power to do so?

I do not believe one can savour a work if one knows nothing of its author, but still less that one can know a writer if one does not first admit that his work gives him away.

In those brief instants which preceded our separation, which both of us knew might be final, we both judged—and when I spoke of our profound agreement on essentials, that is what I meant—that words, cries, laments, sobs and even embraces would weaken what we were exchanging by silence. The control which we were each exerting over ourselves, to reassure the other, and not alarm each other, and which deceived neither of us, was the greatest proof of love we could imagine. In short, if that was to be the last moment of our life as a couple, let it at least keep the dignity that we had tried to give it: thus would each of us carry away the greatest possible picture of the other.

We had always kept silent about the fears, of whatever nature, that we may have had for ourselves. It is joys, not worries, which are good to share.

If such behaviour is stimulating, I certainly agree that it brings in its train a certain fatigue; but that fatigue too is an offering. How moving it is to me now to find traces of it in Colette's letters. Here is what she wrote to a woman friend on March 14, 1944:

"For my part I never tell Maurice about the hours when I say to myself: 'Oh! it's too long and I'm too worn out, I shall be done for before "It" is.' It would sadden him too much. He himself is so wonderfully balanced and firm. We adapt ourselves with a sort of art to this restricted way of living, and our souls do not commit what I call the offence of ill-humour."

It is there that one must seek for Colette's virility and, where her work is concerned, as much in what she refrained from saying as in what she expressed.

On that day there were a thousand arrests. The same evening we slept in the camp at Compiègne, and I learnt only much later that we had reason to congratulate ourselves on this. The Germans had in fact intended to send us straight to Germany, but the French Railways stated that they were not able to arrange transport both for us and for the members of the Wehrmacht going on leave for Christmas, which was drawing near. It was the latter who were chosen.

Except for intense hunger, we had no particular maltreatment to complain of. Our living conditions at Compiègne, compared with what hundreds of thousands of people had to undergo in the German camps, were, at least for people in good health, merely rough and depressing. But against that state of depression we had immediately to organise ourselves, for those who gave in to it were quickly in danger of death.

I have seen so many men eating their hearts out with grief at the thought of the dear ones whom they had left, when for love of them they should have armed themselves against it! Since thenceforward I was able to do nothing for Colette except to survive, I applied my reason and my will to this one purpose. The first thing was to accept the life of the camp as my real life, and to recognise the values which prevailed there as the only ones. Cleanliness, hygiene and good humour became urgent obligations. But the most imperious duty remained that of abolishing the past. As far as was possible I put Colette and our torment out of my thoughts, and by the pang in my heart, which in spite of everything so often took me unawares, I could measure the wisdom of such constraint. Yes, one had to go as far as that!

Since our camp was considered as a camp of reprisals, we had not the right to communicate with our people, and still less to receive parcels from them. I remained for three weeks without news of Colette. And then, little by little, by clandestine ways contacts were re-established. Ah! the first words scribbled by her that I received! My own letters betrayed a sort of food frenzy. In every possible tone of voice I begged for bread and still more bread, for the hunger of the westerner is first and foremost a hunger for bread, and then, in long lists, for fats and other tasty things, long since unobtainable in Paris.

All this while Colette never relaxed her efforts to have me freed. There was no step which she was not prepared to take, no humiliation which she would not face. She saw collaborators and Germans. Who shall blame her? I hope I should have done as much. But a Frenchman, who knew her despair and wished her well, was for all that taken aback by her one day. The man in question was a writer who, having been imprisoned, had regained his liberty by promising the Germans unrestricted collaboration. Apart from the fact that he was amoral and unscrupulous to a staggering degree, he was not lacking in good nature. In any case his only object in going to see Colette was to do her a service.

"I have found the solution for your husband," he said. "I've obtained from 'these gentlemen' a permanent employment for him in the camp of Compiègne. He'll always be well treated and fed."

Colette made a face.

"You haven't any choice, my dear friend. The alternative is death." He knew for certain that our destination sooner or later would be Germany.

Colette gave a start.

"If there is no other way," she said at last, "I'll agree. Is it a very hard job?"

"Not at all. He'll have absolutely nothing to do."

"That's not so bad," said Colette.

"He'll merely give, oh, only from time to time, a few bits of information . . . about his comrades. You see it's a post of trust."

"I refuse," said Colette calmly.

"I don't think I quite understand you, dear friend. Or else you haven't understood what I told you just now. The

other alternative is death. Death, you understand me, death."
And he emphasised the sinister word with one finger on
Colette's table.

"Very well, then, I choose death."

"Not without consulting your husband, I imagine?"

"*We* choose death," amended Colette, not raising her
voice.

He rose with an indignant air and let fall these words,
heavy with blame: "It seems to me, my dear friend, that
you dispose very lightly of the life of a man to whom you
are supposed to be greatly attached."

Whereupon he left, having given this lesson. I do not
know what became of him. I think that at the liberation he
went off to save his skin elsewhere.

The days passed slowly at the camp, very much the same
no doubt as with all such groups in similar conditions. On
the morning of February 6, 1942, I was summoned to the
Germans' office. Apart from two roll-calls a day and exceptional gatherings, the Germans left us to look after our own
discipline, the heads of huts and groups being responsible to
them. I had been the head of a hut for a fortnight, chosen
by the members of it: a summons of this kind as a rule fore-
told a severe reprimand, at the very least.

In the office I found the head of my group and the German sergeant whose job it was to keep an eye on us. Two
other internees were already there. After some verification
of identity the sergeant said: *"Sie sind entlassen."*

I shall never again hear in the German language three
words which will seem sweeter to me.

"What did he say?" asked the two other internees who did not understand German.

"He said that we've been freed."

They were two very sick men, considered as incurable or contagious and who had been discharged. They therefore stood the shock badly and half-fainted: I had to comfort them.

"You have five minutes to get ready," added the sergeant.

With the insolence of one who already felt himself free, I answered: "That's three minutes too many!"

I did not feel very proud as I went up the stairs, my empty suitcase in my hand since I had of course distributed the contents before leaving the camp. I thought it best to ring at the kitchen door and it was Pauline who opened it. She gave a few cries and thought I was not looking well.

"Madame?"

"Madame is at the hairdresser."

I felt disappointed and vaguely relieved. Pauline immediately telephoned to Colette with whom I exchanged a few words. I learned later that Colette, on her way home, had met a woman friend. "Stay with me for a bit," she had said to her, "I daren't go home, I'm afraid." Having prided myself that we had both shown some firmness at my departure, I owe it to myself to admit that I shared this slight cowardice in the face of happiness.

I had in the meantime practically stripped to the skin in the vestibule, so as to prevent the vermin I had on me from getting into the flat, and I had yelled "A bath, a bath!" like Napoleon on returning from Waterloo; but I consider that I had a better right to it since I had not lost any battle.

The heads of huts—everlasting privilege!—had had double rations at Compiègne, so that, with the help of some parcels, I had already regained some of my weight. All the same I had lost twenty-four of the hundred and twenty pounds, without fat, which are my portion. Having a good constitution it did not take me long to regain them and, having got into the way of it, six more which had never been mine before. One risks returning gravely injured from the kind of stay I had just had, but if it is not too prolonged, it can also act as a disintoxicant. At the end of a month I found myself physically absolutely fit. But Colette had suffered more than could be imagined.

The sufferings of the one who departs and the one who remains cannot be compared. The one who runs a danger knows where he stands, the other never. The first has the right to sleep and to relax: Colette had spent long nights of insomnia. She could not regain her nervous equilibrium. I might have been taken again, there was no doubt of it. Rumours of mass arrests were sometimes rife and none of them was kept from her. During her light, uneasy sleep, she would tremble at imaginary rings of the bell. Soon it seemed to me that she absolutely must have a respite, a time when she could stop being on the alert, and the only way I could give her this respite was at the cost of a separation. Thus it was that throughout the whole war I constantly found myself obliged to inflict on her sufferings which I would have given everything in the world to spare her.

I went to take refuge at Saint-Tropez, with friends who had a property situated exactly behind "La Treille Muscate," on the other side of the route des Salins. Dr. Julio Van der Henst, who owes his Christian name to a Mexican mother and his surname to a Dutch father, was an old friend of mine, and it was entirely by chance that we had found ourselves neighbours in the South. His wife, Vera, of Russian origin, lively and sensitive, had belonged to Diaghileff's ballet for a time. We used to see them every day when we were at "La Treille Muscate" and they appear occasionally in silhouette in *La Naissance du Jour*.

Their daughter, Hélène, whom no one has ever called anything but Nouche, had the privilege, when she was a child, of being more directly mentioned in *Journal à Rebours*. Van der Henst's house, almost half-way up the hill, dominated "La Treille Muscate," and from its terrace one could see the whole bay of the Cannebiers. In the old days we used to go up there on moonlight nights with our whole little group of painters, with the Kessels, once or twice with Saint-Exupéry, and others too. How many times have we not dined there, under a dark blue sky, in the sibilant silence of those Provençal nights. Colette would relate astonishing stories and Segonzac adopted his best Berry accent. . . .

I spent a few lazy months at Saint-Tropez. The absence of anxiety, after a long period of threats, was a pleasure in itself but there is none of which one tires more quickly. The same can be said of idleness. All the same I hesitated to return lest Colette should again begin that uneasy watchfulness which had driven me away. But her letters betrayed more and more every day her impatience to have me back. Friends coming from Paris had found her gloomy and saddened: the remedy had proved worse than the disease.

Then came November 11, the landing of the Allies in North Africa and the announcement that the Germans were

occupying the whole country. I decided that I must leave
the coast without delay. The first idea of the Germans would
be to organize a dangerous search there. I neither wanted
to run this risk myself nor to impose it on my hosts. I left
the same day.

But I had to pass the demarcation line and this would
be specially guarded for some time. I decided to break the
journey with some friends in the Tarn, the Lecerfs, who
had invited me there. André Lecerf is the graphologist of
whom Colette speaks in *L'Etoile Vesper*. He is a man of my
age, full of tact, and his wife, a teacher, is as fine as he is.
For the time being he was working single-handed a farm of
about 45 acres, guiding the plough, looking after the oxen
and cramming the geese. My friends gave me the most gen-
erous welcome.

On the journey down, my clandestine passing of the demarcation line had been very carefully prepared from Paris.
For the return, when I judged that the moment had come,
I decided to try my luck in the neighbourhood of Salies-de-
Béarn, and to trust to my inspiration. Not far from the line
I met a French corporal, who examined my rather suspect
papers and asked me what I was doing in those parts. I told
him that I was going to see a relation. He wanted to know
his name. Things were going wrong. Deciding to stake all
on a single throw, I answered that this relation was my wife,
that she lived in Paris, that I was intending to cross the line
without asking permission of anyone whatever, that I would
be grateful if he would help me. He could not go as far as
that, his duty being to put me in prison, but he looked as
if my audacity had pleased him.

"Be off with you," he said, "I haven't seen you."

This was only a first alert. I found some good people who sheltered me for the night and gave me over next morning to a milkman as a guide. We proceeded for a few hundred yards, the milkman, his bottles and I, and reached a dwelling where the milkman stopped. He told me that I could go straight on, that there was no danger, and that there would be no German patrol for an hour. I had not gone fifty yards when I saw the patrol arriving with their rhythmic heavy inexorable tread, polished up to the nines. What to do? It was eight o'clock in the morning. There were only a few peasants idling about and I certainly did not look like one of them. I noticed one of them with an emaciated face and a white moustache. I went up to him, seized his arm and in the tone of one arguing hotly, with lots of gestures, I said: "I tell you, you must sell this field. You simply cannot hesitate. . . ."

By good chance, so as not to be embarrassed by a suitcase, I had put some toilet things and linen into a leather document case. I thus looked quite like a lawyer trying to persuade his client. For the sake of greater precaution, as I was speaking I looked the Germans straight in the eyes. They passed with exasperating slowness. My good peasant had not turned a hair. He merely said, between his teeth, in a weary voice with the delightful local accent:

"I understand. It's 'cos of these chaps shooting the wood pigeons. . . ."

O sweet land of France!

# XXIII

O N MY RETURN to Paris, when the first effervescence of it had died down, I had an idea, worthy perhaps of the ostrich, but which at least secured us quiet nights. They fixed me a "shakedown" under the roof, in a so-called "maid's room." For eighteen months I left Colette every evening at midnight and did not come down from my perch until nine in the morning: we had decided, rather arbitrarily, that at that hour all danger of arrest could be dismissed. The room was hardly more than a garret lit by a narrow fanlight. It was freezing there in winter and baking hot in summer. But I have the gift of being able to sleep in all circumstances; excessive heat or cold induce it equally, and I spent there hours of deep oblivion.

One day followed another, each one tightening the vice of the German occupation and adding to the general penury. It is true that the black market became organised at the same time. It was, for the most part, a not very blameworthy traffic between the countryside and the town. But on other occasions there was connivance with the Germans, as in the case of a little shop in the Palais-Royal, through which tons of sugar and all kinds of victuals passed. But its proprietor had a passion for blue parakeets, of which he had an immense cageful, and for love of those parakeets, which were gorged rather than nourished, Colette could never join in the reprobation with which the neighbourhood overwhelmed their master.

With the landings in Italy, the continual retreat of the Germans in Russia and the preparations of the allies, we were buoyed up with hope which was nourished three times a day by the English radio. But how slow all that was! Colette and I huddled even more closely together. Then came the daily bombing of spring 1944 and then one fine morning—at last!—the landing in Normandy. But patience wears out when one is nearing port, and the two months of marking time in Normandy seemed to us interminable. Finally the map began to move, vast territories were cleared and the Germans began to evacuate their administrative services. Already Paris thought it could hear the rolling thunder of the allied tanks, began to breathe more freely and found it more difficult to contain itself.

I went out as usual on the morning of August 18. The police had been on strike, since the previous night, in revolt against the forces of occupation. On a pillar of the railings at the Louvre, a little handwritten poster incited the Parisians to rise. I crossed the Tuileries and was intending to look down on the Place de la Concorde from the top of the terrace of the Feuillants. After a moment a police car passed containing four or five policemen in plain clothes. When it came abreast of the Orangerie, a German car blocked it. Covered by so many Germans, the Frenchmen had to get out, with their hands up; they were searched and taken away. Five minutes later a big car crammed with French police passed at top speed and veered sharply in front of the Ministère de la Marine with a screech of tyres. A man standing on the running-board fired his revolver in the direction of the Ministry and the car disappeared. Immediately afterwards, two Germans appeared between the columns on the terrace of the Ministry building and mounted a machine-gun there.

Prudence demanded that I should leave, but my curiosity got the better of me; I made up my mind only when the machine-gun started to fire. It was too late. The Germans were evacuating the Tuileries, and asking for papers, and I could not produce mine. I plunged into one of the two big shelters that had been hollowed out under the garden. When I wanted to leave, a quarter of an hour later, the gates of the Tuileries had been shut and the Rue de Rivoli barred. There was nothing to do but to wait for night.

I shared the immense shelter with an old gardener of the Tuileries who, like myself, had taken refuge there, but who had there, in a sort of recess, a kind of bed. I cursed myself heartily; once again I was going to cause Colette anxiety, and this time through my own fault.

I could hear gunfire. Lots of cars and lorries were passing, giving the impression that the Germans were evacuating the town. When night came I said to myself that the liberation of Paris was doubtless a question of hours, and that it would be really too stupid if I were to get myself arrested at the last moment. What worse thing could I inflict on Colette? It was better to go on waiting. The shelter was right opposite the Continental and Meurice hotels, hotels where the Governor of Paris and other important services were lodged.

The Rue de Rivoli was crammed with sentinels. If I were caught climbing railings or jumping trenches, my fate would be settled.

I slept on a chair. The gardener shut himself up in his recess, where he snored like a trumpeter. But before that he had been to look for some tomatoes which grew in the soil covering the shelter. He offered me one of them. It was completely green. I am now able to state that green tomatoes make a very poor meal.

The next day brought no change in our situation. The gardener, shut up in his nook, was taking a sleep cure and I a cure of boredom. When evening came, and I had eaten another tomato, I went through the same prudent reasoning as on the night before. Could I have known that the worst danger was awaiting me? During the night some German soldiers came to sleep in the shelter. I had some of them on each side of me and I dared not even cough: it is a miracle that they did not discover me. With the first light they left and I was dozing on my chair when the cries of my friend the gardener wakened me:

"Comrade, comrade, the gates are open and there are people walking in the garden."

It was the truce which, it will be remembered, was observed for a few hours between the Germans and Paris in revolt.

Colette received me with the growlings of an angry cat, which soon gave way before her tenderness. With the help of some doctor friends, they had searched for me in all the hospitals and first-aid posts of Paris.

I only relate this absurd adventure to punish myself for it.

Those were strange, wavering days which followed. The

German hold on Paris was reduced to a few buildings and some tanks which awkwardly and stealthily patrolled the roads. Paris was stammering the first words of a liberty that she had forgotten, newspapers the size of prospectuses began to appear, and flags were fabricated out of scraps of material. While waiting for the approaching settlement of accounts, the Parisian rediscovered in his long memory the solidarity of the barricades, heroic banter and a smell of gun-powder and sweat.

I turned the knob of the radio: an English speaker was announcing in a moved and solemn voice the liberation of Paris, and inviting the capitals of the whole world to celebrate it. I could not hear the end of the message because of the infernal noise made by a German tank passing with difficulty through the narrow street of the Rue des Petits Champs. It discharged a shot against a house at the corner of the Rue des Petits Pères. The detonation reverberating against the close-set walls made our glass objects tinkle on their shelves and brought down a picture frame. It was obvious that our liberty was not yet in perfect condition. Colette contented herself with saying in a tone of reproach: "What's up with them, are they off their heads?"

Happily they were. On the evening of the 24th Leclerc's tanks came down the Avenue d'Orléans, giving back their voices to all the bells of Paris.

In a very beautiful passage of *L'Etoile Vesper,* Colette has described that evening, "when night rose like a dawn." That evening I saw shining in her eyes tears which in grief she had known so well how to suppress. But the habit of fearing for someone is not so soon lost and she said to me next morning: "I don't believe it, I cannot believe it, it isn't over." All the more because fighting was still going on, there was intermittent gunfire from the roofs and in the deserted Palais-Royal there was nothing to show that anything had changed. When I declared to her that Paris was already full of French and allied troops, she said for a joke: "I shan't really believe it till you've brought a Scottish major here."

"In a kilt?"

"In a kilt."

"I'll go at once."

I crossed the garden. As it happened some British troops were stationed on the Place du Palais-Royal, in front of the Louvre and I ran straight off into the most Scottish of majors, with a kilt and a little tooth-brush moustache. I fell into conversation and he told me that his job was to "re-victual" Paris.

"Good man," I said to him, "we rather need you."

"Yes, but in the meantime I've eaten nothing for twenty-four hours, our cars must have gone astray."

"Don't worry about that. Come and lunch with us. I'll introduce you to my wife."

My success, when I came in with my major, can be imagined. We opened a big tin of corned beef, a gem of the black market kept in reserve for great occasions.

He was indeed a charming Scottish major. When an opportunity arose of telling him that Colette was rather a celebrated French writer, he wanted her name carefully spelled out: "My wife reads a lot," he said, "I expect she'll know."

Then off he went to his obscure duties, kilt, tooth-brush moustache, grateful thanks and all.

Thus it was that we gave hospitality to a Scotsman and,

though deprived of everything, re-victualled the man whose job it was to re-victual us.

But when you awaken from a bad dream you do not forget it entirely. We looked rather like nocturnal animals surprised by the day. During the occupation everyone had developed the habit, on meeting people they knew, if they were not certain of their views, of taking care not to see them. Now we met like certain insects getting in touch through their antennae. Each district counted its heroes, but also its black sheep. Some groups passed, given over to cheerfulness; others, leading women with their heads shaven, looking like hunted animals. Apart from its illustrious black marketeer with the blue parakeets, the Palais-Royal as a whole had behaved well. Madame Laure, an old Russian of great style and unfaltering courage, who lives below us in the flat formerly occupied by Colette, had sheltered parachutists and English airmen. A great friend of animals, with whom she shares her modest resources, she distinguishes the people of the district by their dogs. "The cockers," she said to us, "behaved perfectly during the war, but I could say a lot about the schnauzers."

Those who had left the country came back little by little, bristling with unyielding severity towards weaknesses to which they themselves had not been exposed. Out of a sort of team spirit, we defended against them people for whom in our heart of hearts we had little indulgence. People and things could not reinstate themselves in their former frameworks without a certain amount of creaking.

America, above all New York, at once revealed an intense curiosity about Paris, and particularly concerning the fashions from which it had been separated for five years. Its newspaper correspondents fell upon everything which seemed to them characteristic of Paris and of France. I realised how much the fame of Colette had increased abroad, although nothing that she had written or done had been known outside. Separation can sometimes displace the poles of attraction in a quite unforeseen way. Louis Jouvet told us that, during his five years of voluntary exile, if he thought of Paris it was to wish himself suddenly transported in front of the shop-windows of Hermès. For certain Americans their nostalgia for Paris fixed itself on Colette. At that time this was true only of a very Europeanised élite. It was periodicals devoted to women, like *Vogue* and *Harper's Bazaar* which asked her for articles. *Harper's Bazaar* translated and published *Gigi, Harper's Bazaar* whose directress, Carmel Snow, said to me the year after with a strong American accent: "Without Dior, France would be done for!"

The books of Colette which appeared during the war are above all works of imagination: the stories collected in *Chambre d'Hôtel, Le Képi, Gigi,* and her last novel: *Julie de Carneilhan.* Concise, nervous, spare, they betray no weakness. The story called *Gigi* may be considered as Colette's last romantic production. After an interval of forty years this little character Gigi took her place beside Claudine, Colette's first creation. Her success was no less and appears to be as lasting. Between those two young girls lies a work which by its richness and diversity forms a world. *Claudine à l'Ecole* is three hundred pages long, *Gigi* contains barely eighty. What their author lost in freshness and abundance she gained in power and mastery. *Gigi* is a *tour de force* which demands an art, a craft that no first book could offer.

Sketched in sure, incisive lines, five strongly marked characters develop at their ease in these few pages, not a word of which could possibly, it seems, be cut or altered.

The fact that, after *Gigi*, Colette created no more characters was deliberate. "After seventy," she said to me, "the mind loses the force necessary to invent and sustain a character to the end. It is time for me to give this up."

The years 1944 and 1945 marked a profound change in her. That disease, arthritis of the hip, which had for so long been making its way within her, was now installed. From then on she had to reckon with pain, and soon with old age. Faithful to herself, Colette looked them in the face, or better still, took them as objects for her curiosity.

That is why to speak of her resignation does not go far enough. She had decided to draw from her ills what compensations they could offer, to observe them and to exert her own perseverance where they were concerned. If any were to doubt this, the proof of it would be furnished by *L'Enfant Malade,* a link between the fiction in Colette's work and the new manner that she was to adopt, half souvenirs, half journal. This fairy-tale is a pendant to *L'Enfant et Les Sortilèges.*

The sick child has lost the use of his two legs and has created for himself an imaginary world which offers him all the escape he desires. To this end he distorts the objects close at hand, rides upon a paper-knife, sails upon a rose, lands, returns, and visits enchanted countries. This universe which is for him alone, and the objects which are his slaves, he cherishes to such a point that he can hardly resign himself to getting well and only agrees to it with regret. Here is the passage which ends these pages:

"Jean makes a sign in farewell to his reflection with the angel's locks, which returns his greeting from the far side of an earthly night deprived of marvels, the only night allowed to children whom death has released and who fall asleep consenting, cured and disappointed."

In 1944 Colette was still walking, although with difficulty. *L'Enfant Malade* foreshadows immobility, just as *La Naissance du Jour* foreshadowed the renunciation of love. I could not have known anything about it at the time when that story was written. I asked myself what were her sources, or what necessity impelled her. Could I have supposed that Colette was projecting on to paper a still distant future, imagining the defence that she would oppose to it and knew already that one day she would come to prefer her illness to any cure?

Nearly ten years later, tied to her divan-bed, Colette wrote:

"From my ceiling, a scarlet sky with a wide white moulding, there still rain clouds, a bird and lightning, which I deserve: those trammelled as I am are not deprived of help." And in *Le Fanal Bleu:* "Luckily I have pain."

It will be seen one day—it can be seen now—that there is a universe of Colette just as there is one of Balzac and one of Proust, that practically nothing in it can be taken away from the rest, that it offers a perfectly original and coherent view of reality in all its dimensions, a tonic climate to which one must constantly return to get courage to live, and finally that it has been conceived by an exceptional woman, so much so that it is no use hoping that the combination of circumstances which formed her can ever be repeated.

For five years Colette, the country woman, had not left Paris. Because she could not go there she had sold Méré, and we no longer had a corner of the country for ourselves. Easter 1945 offered her her first escape, thanks to an invitation from Simone Berriau who owns at Les Salins d'Hyères, in the Var, a property called "Mauvannes," where every Parisian who is at all Parisian has been or stayed. It is an ancient farm, turned into a vast and comfortable living place, with vineyards which produce a wine that has gained a reputation, the sea a hundred yards away, and salt pans glittering in the sun; but its principal attraction is none the less its astonishing hostess with her smiling welcome. This white and brown Norman, beautiful as the day, landed one day from Morocco, resolved to conquer Paris. She decided, without having any preparation for it, to sing at the Opéra Comique and she sang in leading rôles there. Another time she went to have a tooth seen to and married the dentist, for a time at any rate. She wanted to be a film star, made a film which did not succeed, and another which ran for a long time. Finally she longed for a theatre, got the Théatre Antoine, became an influential manageress and put on Sartre and all the best authors.

The first time she met Colette she stormed her as if she were a redoubt. Colette loved watching her live, marvelling at her energy, her assurance and her audacities. "Mauvannes" was like a marshalling yard, a halt, a posting house. No one, not even the mistress of the house, knew in advance who would be there for meals or who would spend the night there. She kept open house, and on a splendid scale.

We stayed there ten days, and went there again in August. Slightly stunned by the noisy gaiety which reigned there, Colette abandoned herself to that easy life, astonished and amused by the dazzle of it. There, in an atmosphere of a popular fair, she finished *L'Etoile Vesper*, that contemplative book stamped with serenity. To pass the time I wrote, with Yves Mirande, a play, *Pas un Mot à La Reine-Mère*, which was performed the following winter. Mirande is almost the contemporary of Colette. An old Parisian of Breton stock, in our troubled world he upholds the rights of frivolity. A man of the theatre to his finger-tips, he has written twenty plays which have been hits, and related the story of a hundred others which would have been even more so. He never says no, not wanting to hurt anyone, and thereafter trusts in God to get himself out of his contradictory promises. Colette and he used to meet in the old days in newspaper offices, and at first nights, and they treated each other familiarly like old comrades.

*L'Etoile Vesper* was published in Switzerland in fulfilment of a contract made during the war. *Mes Apprentissages*, evoking a past which had left Colette with some bitterness, was a brilliant, lucid book. *L'Etoile Vesper*, another volume of souvenirs, radiates an unparalleled human warmth. In it Colette, becoming little by little hampered in her movements, begins to count the treasures scattered around her, and to establish that enchanted world which was to serve her as a setting when she quitted this life. Having reached a pinnacle which allowed her to be detached she drew from it a smiling indulgence, and a tender humour.

Never had her vocabulary been more subtle, nor her phrasing more supple.

*L'Etoile Vesper* was born in deplorable conditions. The book was put on sale on July 14 in a deserted Paris, without any attempt to call the attention of the public to its appearance. For all that the public discovered it, but because of a quota system of distribution between France and Switzerland, the publisher had only been able to send in 10,000 copies, which were quickly snapped up. When a new quota crossed the frontier six months later, the buyers had grown tired of their vain quest, so that what is perhaps the most moving of Colette's books is also the one which, to this day, has had the smallest circulation.

She had resolved never to refuse an inscription, since she could not see any way of discriminating. This occupation ate up a part of her time, for piles of books were dumped on us. She sometimes used to speculate on the real motives of what has become a collective mania, a contagion which seems to be universal. The mad galloping of youth to stalk the stars of the theatre or the films derives from the hunt. During Colette's last public appearances, people would pick up dirty scraps of paper from the ground to get her to sign them. They would stop her in the road and bar her passage.

The ones who brought a book generally asked for "a personal inscription" and Colette took infinite trouble over it. But sometimes she yielded to a touch of irritation and wrote: "To Monsieur X, whom I do not know." But there was never a case when the beneficiary of this rebuff did not receive it with joy: at last he had it, his personal inscription!

In June 1946, I took Colette to Uriage: we simply had to try something. One day when she was resting after her rather tiring cure, I saw two well-dressed ladies arriving and carrying a heavy suitcase crammed with books.

"They're for inscriptions," they said, whereupon they sat down.

"I'm afraid I must ask you to come back, it needs a certain time to—"

"But we are living in a château, which isn't very near here."

All the same they agreed to allow me some time, though with a bad grace.

Colette accomplished this imposition with conscience, taking the necessary time over it and affixing signatures and inscriptions, some of which were full of pith. When the two ladies returned they examined the inscriptions one by one in silence, not a single feature moving. Finally one of them opened a mean mouth to say: "We hoped for something better."

And off they went with their load, very disgruntled. They sent neither a flower nor a word of thanks.

Some readers nowadays consider that an inscription is a tribute that one can exact from a writer, merely because one has bought his book. I have even seen unknown people trying to dictate to Colette what she ought to write: "What I would like would be if you were to put: 'To my dearest friend. . . .'"

# XXIV

I^T WAS IN 1945 that Colette was unanimously elected to
the Académie Goncourt. As long as she was able to go
to the luncheons at which the members met every month,
she greatly looked forward to them. She felt herself surrounded there with a solicitude which touched her: "It's all
very well my posing as an old bachelor," she wrote, "it's still
a very feminine pleasure that I get out of being the only
woman at the Goncourt luncheons, surrounded with an
areopagus of men." She loved her colleagues with a tender
camaraderie and called them "my little Goncourts." When
Lucien Descaves died in 1949, the Goncourt elected Colette
President. Honours surprised her, but she was not indifferent to them. This, above all others, made her proud.

Sometimes the Goncourts came to her flat in a body and
gathered around her divan-bed. "Closer, closer," she would
say. "Sit on my feet."

Literature took a back seat on those occasions, the pleasure
of the company was all that mattered. For Colette's eightieth
birthday the luncheon took place in her flat, without her
having to do anything about it: a wave of a magic wand

brought to her house the Restaurant Drouant and all its apparatus, even down to the traditional cake with eighty candles.

The Goncourts retain a lively and tender memory of their President.

Even after I have shown Colette in the ardour of her activity, in the vivacity of her daily life, in her mobility and her acuteness, in the passionate attention she paid to things, in her scrupulousness and her laborious patience, in her ability and her restraint, even after I have spoken of her unparalleled gifts, of her genius and her lofty virtues so well concealed, I shall not have revealed her in her entirety if I do not make up my mind to say that before everything else she was love. How full of tenderness she was and how she tried to resist it! Her grumpy tone, her surly air, her brusqueness and her humour were chiefly useful to her in helping her not to melt at every moment.

She would have liked that not to have been known, nor how attached she was to people, nor the impulse which made her reach out to everything that lives, suffers, loses courage, and falters. But would that murmur of love which, at the end of her life, came from the ends of the world to beat against her door have arisen if all the humble people of the world had not perceived by mysterious ways how much she loved them?

There are people whom all her life she helped and encouraged, keeping their heads above water. When her correspondence is published it will furnish touching examples of this.

Renée Hamon, a young woman of Breton stock, had in-

herited a stubborn liking for the sea, and for adventure.
Furnished with slender resources and a courage which nothing could daunt, she used to go off alone to distant countries,
explore them on a bicycle and return with only one idea, to
go off again. She was a blond and though very tiny she
was well-built though her head, which she held high and
proudly, was perhaps rather big for her body. She wrote to
Colette, was invited to go and see her, and knew how to
touch her. Thenceforward Colette spared herself no pains to
help her accomplish her desire. She wrote to ministers and
directors of newspapers, got subsidies for her, and commis-
sions for articles, showed her how to do them, encouraged
her to write a book, undertook to find a publisher for it,
prefaced it, and introduced her to radio listeners:

"We must get to know the name of Renée Hamon too, a
slip of a woman who got into her head a few months back
to go and see the other side of the world. All alone, and
with a purse as light as her luggage, she set off. She is here,
waiting her turn, looking like a thin cat with beautiful eyes
and thick hair. She is afraid neither of God, nor the Devil,
nor Man, nor murderous climates, nor of crossing the Pa-
cific on a schooner with not a single other woman or white
person on board; nor of doing the cooking for a Tahitian
crew and scrubbing the bridge. There is only one thing in
the world which she fears: speaking before the micro-
phone . . ."

When Renée had succeeded in getting off again, Colette
wrote to her, in 1937:

I've received your letter safely, my little corsair, and the
two photos. When I saw the one that shows you stranded
on your luggage on the edge of those distant sands, I

couldn't prevent a feeling of alarm and also a kind of envy. The jealousy of a duck with clipped wings, who sees the green-necks flying over the pond. . . .

But there was pity in it too. You look very much alone and very small on that sandy waste and under that feathery palm. Yet I know that you meet any sea wind with that Breton head of yours thrown back and that, as you say, "the further off it is the more beautiful." You are like those fishermen of Sauzon (I lived in Belle-Isle for a summer long ago) who could never wait for the end of an exceptionally long storm. They got so bored on land that they went to sea again contrary to reason. . . .

This time, in addition to shells, dried flowers, native costumes, and photographs, you must bring back a book.

Renée Hamon kept a diary which is merely one long paean to Colette, a daily act of devotion. In between two pieces of reporting, which Colette placed in periodicals for her, she lived in a little house at Trinité-sur-Mer in the Morbihan, which she called "Moana." In February 1939, during a very mild winter season, our whole household, animals and all, went to spend ten days with her. Since her "hut" was too small, we stayed at Auray. Colette could not have given Renée a greater pleasure.

Young though she still was, she was attacked during the war with an incurable disease. Knowing already that Renée was done for, Colette hastened the publication of her book: *Amants de L'Aventure*. From then on the whole aim of Colette's letters was to give her hope:

28 July 1943.

My dear little Renée, at last I have your book. Not the one which I am sure your own hand has inscribed for me,

but a copy "like everyone else," which bears only its printed
dedication—a beautiful dedication, my child, I shall never
have another which touches my heart so deeply. How I
should have liked to celebrate the book's appearance by a
little lunch *à la beaujolaise,* washed down by a little champagne . . . That will be for later. We'll wait for you.

Don't torment yourself about your book: it is good. It is
as it ought to be, it has, thank goodness, the unevennesses
which help to give it individuality and a personality. Shall
I say that it resembles you? Yes, I will say it, at the risk of
making you vain. It has the taste, the colour, the inimitable
ring of real things. I no more want to see it more polished
than I want to endow you with a Greek nose and smooth
bands of hair.

Just as I'm writing, here comes the copy that you've sent
me. Why naturally, my corsair! One of these days you must
certainly get under way again. May you once more be that
little effigy of adventure, upright on a boat, with a sail behind you like a wing! You've got a hard row to hoe to get
there. . . . On the 27th it was the feast day of Sainte Anne
d'Auray, wasn't it? You must have thought of her, and I
was thinking of you.

Renée Hamon died at the end of October, in Brittany. A
man friend, very much older than she, had been her companion during the last years of her life, and helped during
her final illness. It was to him that Colette wrote this letter,
whose measured tone only makes its emotion the more apparent:

If I'm writing to you it is not because I want to write to
you, it is because you are so much part of my most constant,
I might say my most urgent, thoughts. I know very well

that that poor child had to die, that it was indispensable, desirable and that there was no other salvation. But that doesn't prevent me, now that it is all over, from feeling rebellious, as we all are.

I think of you, as I have been thinking all this time, with admiration. You have avoided nothing and neglected nothing; your letter which you took such affectionate care to see that I got as quickly as possible is, whether you like it or not, one of the moving letters that I have received in my life. . . .

If I become unsociable and silent when I am not happy, it is because I rely on silence and unsociability to help me.

To-day is Saturday. Perhaps you are still down there. What you are doing is the task of a brave man. As I think of it, I remember that it was here you met that little creature, so solitary, who has died without hurting anyone and on whom there was no real blemish. She had a coat like the plumage of the grebe, which remains always spotless. You took everything on your shoulders. Small though she was the total weight of a person one wants to be happy is a weight indeed. All things that you touch since her death are memories still warm and which chafe, even that little house which owes it to you that it's standing up.

I expect that when you and I see each other again we shall be very calm. I have always taken immense trouble not to show emotion, and most of the time I have succeeded. But I cannot refuse myself the sad pleasure of telling you of the grief I feel. If by chance you bring back from there things that you think you ought to hand to me, be kind enough to keep them for a while. I do not need them, what I do need is not to see them at this moment. Now that is said and you will find me looking just as usual. . . .

In Colette's correspondence other examples will be found of devotion on one side and active and protective tenderness on the other. But her friendship with Renée Hamon is bathed in its own poetry. Colette sent Renée in her stead to those coloured countries of which she had dreamt so much: "You shall have them, those islands of yours!" she wrote to her while she was fighting to get help and subsidies for her. Every winter Renée used to send Colette wild daphnes, modest and scented flowers found only in Brittany, for which Colette kept a certain nostalgia. From her voyages she brought her back shells of new shapes and colours. Daphnes and shells became part of the fairy-world of Colette.

After her cure at Uriage in 1946 we went down to Grasse, invited by our friends the Charles de Polignacs, who used to rent a country house there in the summer called "Les Aspres." We returned there for the whole of our holidays in 1948, and again in 1949, but by then the Polignacs had bought a property, this time west rather than south of Grasse, called "Le Mas." We were greatly attached to them. In addition to elegance of manners, which is only a trimming and would not have been enough to hold Colette, they have in the highest degree elegance of the heart, and there was nothing to which Colette was more sensitive. Pata de Polignac went to see Colette nearly every day, knocking at her door with a gay and imperious rap, and however, tired she was, Colette relaxed with her, abandoning herself to the authoritative care of her friend and smiling at her beautiful face. Charles de Polignac often came to rejoin his wife: this former cavalry officer from Saumur had been the friend of Ségalen, of Gilbert de Voisins, of Jean Giraudoux and of

Edmond Jaloux. Sometimes they were accompanied by
Prince Pierre de Monaco, who had been a Polignac before
his marriage and who was the father of Prince Rainier III.
Under a haughty exterior he concealed a wide knowledge
and a warmth of heart which was stifled because of his
inability to show it. Colette saw through this and cherished
a considerable friendship for him. Reserved ways no more
deceived her about the quality of one person than a seductive
outside deceived her about the inanity of another.

When she had given her friendship she never took it back,
but it was impossible for her not to remain clear-sighted
about the defects of her friends. Her need of identification
was too great for that. Not in the least biassed, or at any rate
biassed with her eyes open, she could remain partial but she
could not delude herself. One day I thought I ought to reveal to her a mean thing which one of her women friends
had done to her.

"D'you think I don't know it?" she said to me. And she
added: "Poor thing!"

There were many things that she did not know, but she
never knew anything superficially. Such habits of investigation might have made her dry or disillusioned. On the contrary she kept her freshness intact to the very end. But it was
the real which seemed to her fantastic, inexhaustibly fantastic. To know a subject thoroughly does not prevent it
from being different the next moment, seen under another
light or in a different relation with what surrounds it.

"It doesn't bore you," I said to her one day when we
were going for a walk, "to go back by the same road?"

"It isn't the same road, since we're going in the opposite
direction."

She had no basic scepticism. She used to tell fortunes, her own and that of others, with cards, and in former days was always glad to accompany her friends to fortune tellers and other foretellers of the future.

"Do you believe in it then?" I asked her.

"No, but it amuses me just the same. For me it is rather like paper-weights." Everyone knows the liking she had for paper-weights because of the little innocent and coloured mystery that they enclose.

It has sometimes been suggested that she was anti-clerical, which is absurd. Her attitude was not "anti" anything. François Mauriac gave her the Epistles of St. Paul and the Gospels. She read them with a great deal of interest like beautiful stories. She would even sometimes go and light a candle at Notre Dame des Victoires. But she also held a gold coin in her left hand whenever she ate pancakes on Shrove Tuesday, as people did in her part of the country. Superstition? No, paper-weights. Her faith and her fervour, both most lively, were entirely reserved for what was within reach of her hand, and to know it better was to believe in it better.

There was the marriage of Pauline. Pauline was so much a part of our life that, just as Colette did, I have spoken of her as though everyone must know her: the moment has come for a more formal introduction. Pauline was thirteen years old when, a little peasant girl from the neighbourhood of Brive, she entered Colette's service during one of the latter's visits to Castel-Novel, the château of the Jouvenels in the Corrèze. Very dark and with an olive complexion, and big slightly protruding yellow eyes, she must have looked like a young wild cat. She remained with Colette for nearly forty years. From a shy little servant with unexpected moods she became, as the years went by, that guardian angel, that ever-helping arm on whose support Colette relied at every moment of the day and night. She gave to the word serve its most noble meaning by claiming the privilege with the same proud humility as knights did for their lady in former days. She has never had any other horizon than Colette and has never served nor ever will serve any other master. It is true that Pauline to-day is in my service, but it is always Colette whom she serves, and I find it good that it should be thus.

For all that, Pauline had a secret: for a long time she had been engaged without Colette's being aware of it. But she declared that she would only get married if Colette agreed to it, and that she intended in any case that it should not get in the way of her service. It must be said that Colette had shown the same consideration for Pauline, at the time when she married me:

"What do you think of it, Pauline?"

Pauline had reflected and answered: "Well, he isn't bad!"

The marriage took place in November 1946. Colette was Pauline's witness both at the *Mairie* and the Church of St. Roch. But the great affair was the lunch. Pauline's husband, a big, red-faced, placid fellow, more sensitive than he looked and whom Colette called "my son-in-law," had a sister who was a baker at Clichy: the wedding feast took place in the bakehouse of the bakery. Pauline comes from the Limousine and her husband from Auvergne and both of them have a great many relations. At that time none of the restrictions had been relaxed and the shortages were still great. But the guests, some of whom came from the Corrèze and some from

the Cantal, showed what the French peasantry can do when
it is on its mettle: each one of them had brought at least a
leg of mutton and another piece of meat or venison. In the
warm bakehouse with its vaulted roof, under the dancing
gleams of a great blazing fire, there took place, between one
o'clock and six in the evening, a bewildering procession of
joints and poultry, sometimes interspersed with a water-ice
or a *"trou normand,"* * a repast such as Jordaens would have
arranged, and such as no bourgeois, princely or royal household could have provided. When Colette, her daughter, a
few of our closest friends and I finally retired, walking heavily, the other guests had just decided that they would rest
for an hour where they were . . . before dining!

* I.e., a glass of Calvados, by way of helping the digestion to prepare for
a further onslaught.

# XXV

In 1948 the *Oeuvres Complètes* of Colette began to appear. This moment, which should establish the definite dimensions of his work, is a serious one for an author. Everything that he has written for every kind of reason, impelled by necessity, circumstances and sometimes chance, is going to appear for the first time as a whole, not only in the eyes of the public but in his own. If the materials he has used are too light they will not support this massive structure. But it may also be that without the writer's being aware of it, those scattered efforts have ended by forming a complete work, those dissimilar texts, interacting on each other and consolidating themselves, offer a harmonious and coherent whole, an image of the universe in which the race to come will seek its own image.

It is a time too for putting things in order which, for Colette, was particularly necessary. Going as she did from one publisher to another, and always oppressed by the need for money, her books are frequently collections of chronicles and stories put together from everything she could lay hands on. Some texts appear by mistake in two different books.

The reputation of many a writer would have foundered in such a hotchpotch.

I had spent nearly three years in establishing these *Oeuvres Complètes*, hunting out and grouping together unpublished texts, eliminating from each volume what had appeared elsewhere, writing bibliographical notices which sorted out the tangle of successive editions. Colette re-read and corrected all the texts, adding to them a certain number of short prefaces. I had a great deal of difficulty in preventing her from using the scissors too briskly on her first writings. It is by no means certain that an author is the best judge of his work, any more than a painter is. Merely because they have developed they have a tendency to repudiate their early manner and to touch up things whose value for us lies precisely in a certain lack of art, compensated by freshness and spontaneity. To the classic question: "Which of your books do you think the best?" Colette sometimes answered:

"The one I haven't written yet."

She made heavy cuts, particularly in *La Chambre Eclairée* and in *Les Heures Longues* and refused many texts, not yet published in book form, that I submitted to her. Even if a number of these pages seem to me to-day to have been unjustly put aside, they cannot appear without the public's being warned that the author did not pass them.

Colette corrected in this way some thousands of pages. She would pause to say to me: "Have I really written all that? Maurice, is it possible that I've written all that?"

Sometimes she would make sufficiently bold to say: "It's not so badly done, this work, you know!"

I knew.

Many well-read people, both in France and abroad, only gave Colette the rank which she deserves from the moment of this publication. More than one remained astonished that a work so little thought out, so subject to caprice, could, while tackling such a diversity of subjects, offer such unity, with never a weakening in the writing, or any self-satisfaction on the part of the author.

During this time her name became better known among the great public, thanks to the screen. The cinema had hitherto only paid a casual attention to the work of Colette: a *Vagabonde* before 1930, a *Claudine à l'Ecole* about 1937, both mediocre products. In 1945 Pathé grudgingly bought the film rights of *Gigi,* but could not make up their minds to use them. "Colette? Yes, of course, Colette, but what has she done in the cinema?" So Pathé considered it a godsend when another film company offered three years later to buy from them the rights in question. These pioneers had let themselves be persuaded, though without conviction, by the producer Jacqueline Audry. The film came out obscurely in the provinces, and immediately surprising results were announced: long queues were forming in front of the cinemas where it was being shown. The producer could not understand it.

"Let's see now," he said, "my star—Danièle Delorme—is unknown, and my director not much more. Whatever can be the reason for this triumph? Who can be my unknown star? Ah! I know, it must be Colette!"

Going from one extreme to the other he summoned me to his offices, ready to buy indiscriminately the rights of everything that Colette had written. And since there are no people so gregarious as film producers, others followed his example. From one day to the next the cinema had become "Colette conscious" and it has remained so. So far six films have been taken from her works and three more will be soon.

The years 1948–50 marked a veritable discovery of Colette by every kind of public, speaking every kind of tongue. I am ready to agree that part of the reason for this was that her affairs were now better organised. When, after the war, I was about to launch out into all sorts of enterprises, it seemed to me that the task of making the work of Colette better known ought for me to take precedence over any other project. I knew very well that her powers were doomed to a slow decline. My place thenceforward was at her side. I would strive to see that her work received the greatest consideration possible, and her person those honours of which I judged that none could be too great for her. And if at the same time it were given to me, while mounting at her side a guard each day more vigilant and anticipating her unexpressed wishes, to help her, when the moment came, to take leave, without shock or bitterness, of a life harmoniously accomplished, would I not have fulfilled a destiny that any man might envy? I feel sure that we should be grateful to people less for what they give us than for what they allow us to devote to them.

Colette's work was still far from being appreciated at its true worth abroad. The multiplicity of her French publishers was the reason for this, since each one of them could only deal with a few of her books. I suggested to them that they should group in my hands what had hitherto been dispersed, leaving me to choose in each country an exclusive publisher who would undertake to bring out successively all the books of Colette with a care worthy of so vast a trust. Thus it is that in England, in America, and in Germany, very beautiful editions of the works of Colette are appearing.

The war had given rise to a literature of despair. A sort of nihilism prevailed in ideas and attitudes, a black realism which turned its back on reality, made of a play of light and shade. But you cannot keep youth for long in a climate of gloom. The new adherents to the work of Colette were the young who, on emerging from a long tunnel, discovered her like the call of fresh air. Through her they found again those deep sources which people had told them were dried up, a picture of the world which hid neither its deficiencies nor its beauties, and a quest for the authentic which is in itself a reason for living.

Through her work these new readers divined the true Colette, her modesty, her innocence, her gentleness, and they dedicated their hearts to her. From the four corners of the earth they sent her their messages, too numerous soon for her to answer them all, a fact which distressed her. I can only give a feeble idea of this movement of love which went on growing right up to Colette's death. More and more was attention fixed on that window, beside a garden that once was royal, where a woman of genius was soon to glow with her last fires.

Dazzling revival of the play *Chéri,* first performance of *Gigi* on Broadway, films, adaptations for the radio, new translations; and while her work was attaining ever loftier heights, its author was wisely limiting her own horizon. In 1949 appeared *Le Fanal Bleu* and *Pour un Herbier,* which was born of an idea suggested by Mermod, the Lausanne

publisher: "Once or twice a week, for a year or more, I shall
send you some flowers," he wrote. "When you feel like it you
will trace the portrait of one of these flowers. And then we
will make a little volume of them."

Colette could not resist such a siren's lure as that. In all
her labours she had never hitherto trodden such a flowery
path. The bouquets were received with transports. The delicious little book reflects the well-being which dictated it.
Later on Mermod brought out an illustrated edition of it,
the drawings for which he entrusted to Raoul Dufy. The
meeting between Colette and Dufy was a meeting between
two kindred sensibilities. Often, towards the end, Colette
asked me for that book to look at again.

The copyright of *Pour un Herbier* belongs to Mermod,
who has so far only published some limited editions of it. I
hope that he may soon bring out an edition at a price
within reach of a wide public, for few of Colette's works
are so delightful.

*Le Fanal Bleu* was written between 1946 and 1948. It is
the same type of book as *L'Etoile Vesper,* half journal, half
souvenirs. The contrast between those two titles marks well
the difference between the two books themselves. If the star
still illuminates the world, the blue lantern throws its light
on the objects within its own orbit. But the paler light has
not made Colette's sight less keen. The journey round the
room remains an exploration. And two pages of *Le Fanal
Bleu* on household objects have given haberdashery an eter-
nal place among poetic subjects.

Nor is it the influence of the evening star which gives the
greater serenity. *L'Etoile Vesper* ends on this pessimistic
note: ". . . I see from here the end of the road." Three years

later, in the midst of agonising suffering and with declining
powers, the author ended: "Once upon a time I thought it
was the same with writing as with other jobs: when you've
downed the tools you cry joyfully 'Finished!' and brush your
hands from which rain grains of a sand one had thought
precious. . . . That is the moment when in the shapes that
these grains of sand write, one reads the words 'To be continued. . . .' "

*Le Fanal Bleu* is in truth her last book. *En Pays Connu,*
which appeared in 1951, is only a collection of unpublished
pieces, which appeared in a limited edition in the *Oeuvres
Complètes.* After *Le Fanal Bleu,* and before Colette began
to trace for her own sake those exercises, that loom of Pe-
nelope, of which I have spoken, there were two short essays:
*"Ces Dames anciennes,"* and *"Gîte d'écrivain,"* which were
published under the title *"Derniers Ecrits,"* in the post-
humous volume *Belles Saisons,* and also some occasional
pieces. The occasion for the last in date of these was an album of photographs, *Paradis Terrestre.* Contrary to what
normally happens with this kind of album, instead of the
text being a commentary on the photographs, it was the
photographer, Izis, who set out to discover the landscapes
and animals described in *En Pays Connu.* He had to lie in
wait for long periods in the forest of Rambouillet and the
park at Clères . . . In spite of the care which Izis took to
follow Colette's text exactly, in the end a few connecting
pages were needed to ensure the equilibrium of the volume,
and these he asked Colette to write. They deserve to be detached from their context to show that the hand of their
author at eighty is as firm and her observation as penetrating

as ever. Here are two extracts. The first accompanies the
picture of a hind swimming across a pool:

> . . . The creature which he [the photographer] was waiting
> for had given him a rendezvous. In the middle of a glossy
> page she swims from west to east, breaking up the glittering
> ripples set up by the rhythm of her invisible legs. Her blond
> head on her close-cropped neck, her divergent ears, the man
> lying in wait has captured it all. But doubtless he had not
> hoped—did he deserve it?—that all around the swimming
> creature there would spread a trail of light, from which
> would emerge her neck, her profile, her almond eye, and a
> single nostril . . . Don't be afraid. You can easily see from
> that robe of light spread upon the water all around this
> creature that swims so marvellously, from all that you can
> see, that she is neither doe nor fawn, but simply a fairy.

Another photograph shows a head of a doe rising out of
a clump of tall ferns:

> The thrust of her forehead now opens up an undergrowth
> which is all of fern. But how can we understand or accept
> the dimensions of such a forehead, and the distance sepa-
> rating one eye from the other. Let us not accept them. Let
> us even deny that immediately below the cornet of the
> ear, the fur of the ear, the velvet of the ear, there starts and
> continues a blond stretch which does not belong to the fern,
> to the ocean of ferns, to their spore cases trampled by violent
> hoofs. Here the bracken reigns. Put no trust in that mag-
> nificent head which, a stranger to the bracken, dominates
> the top of the page. *Elle ne fait que feindre de fendre la
> fougère.*

Perhaps some will blame these lines for an excess of vir-
tuosity; too assured a handling of the vocabulary. Certainly

*"Elle ne fait que feindre de fendre la fougère"* is a deliberate effect. But: *"Pour qui sont ces serpents qui sifflent sur
vos têtes"* * is no less so. There is many a writer who would
be happy to incur such blame one day.

These were for Colette years of keen physical suffering
made worse by her efforts to retain some mobility. Only
when she had to resign herself to not moving any longer
did the suffering diminish. First one stick, then two, then
a wheel-chair for out-of-doors, and finally a wheel-chair for
moving about the house; this disease of arthritis proceeds
like the serpent which, to make its grip more sure, encircles
its victim with an unhurried coil and then another, and
still another.

At no time did Colette agree to take sedatives. It was not
that she feared the effect of them on her general condition.
It was merely that her liking for authenticity was against
it: "Aspirin," she said to me, "changes the colour of my
thoughts. It makes me gloomy. I would rather suffer cheer-
fully."

She said also: "I want to know just how far I can go."

This pain became the object of her untiring curiosity, the
food for those challenges that she loved to launch at herself.
To mask it would have seemed to her like a proposal to
change the time or tamper with the compass.

It was in 1950 that we went to Monte Carlo for the first
time. The pretext was that a doctor there claimed that he
could cure arthritis of the hip by injections. Our stay at
Geneva in 1946 had had the same motive, but there it was

* From Racine's *Andromaque*.

we who tried to persuade a doctor, described as miraculous, that he cured arthritis, and he seemed very afraid of the responsibility that we were inflicting on him. He was a fat man, overworked and breathless, to whom Colette, while he was treating her, gave a great deal of very sensible medical advice.

We returned five years running to Monte Carlo, for sojourns that became longer and longer. People were astonished by this, as they were later on by our summers at Deauville, for these are hardly country places. Had Colette fallen a victim to snobism and the desire to show herself?

The truth was that convenience alone guided our decisions; my life and Colette's thenceforward revolved round that increasing powerlessness whose effects we had to palliate and delay. My ingenuity and Colette's patience had no other employment.

During a certain time it was still possible for her, with the help of my arm or Pauline's, to climb or descend the stairs, and then she had to give it up. After that a sedan-chair, a contraption made of tubes which we fixed to her wheel-chair with straps, and the help of two men, enabled her to go up and down, though dangerously. Minutely calculated movements allowed Colette to get into her car and go for a drive. These manoeuvres were not simple and since there was no possibility of constructing a lift in the Rue de Beaujolais, I considered for some time exchanging our apartment for a ground-floor one. But Colette and the Palais-Royal were already inseparable. It was better to take long holidays in hotels which had rooms on the ground-floor and where Colette could at least come and go without hindrance.

The airplane was the sole means of transport which was

still permitted to her: a journey in a car, because of the sitting position, became too tiring, and as for trains, Colette could not possibly have got along the corridors. Our transport demanded a complete organisation, which began in Colette's bedroom in Paris. There had to be one chair here, another there, two men at one point, four somewhere else. The car would follow by road, and Pauline, who refuses to fly, would take the Blue Train so as to be with her mistress sooner.

The airport at Nice was notified each time of Colette's arrival, and journalists and flowers awaited her. On one occasion the Mayor of Nice, Monsieur Médecin, an important person, came to bid her welcome and introduce himself to her.

"I am Médecin," he said.

"Thank you, Doctor," answered Colette, who was not much used to political personages, "but I am in quite good health for the moment!"

For five years we stayed in the Hotel de Paris, in the same ground-floor suite, consisting of two bedrooms, a drawing-room, and a room for Pauline. It had a view over the esplanade garden where Colette spent long hours enjoying the blue sky, and the feeling of the sun and the pure air on her skin.

In the State of Monaco there is neither industry, nor commerce, nor agriculture, nor grazing and one may look in vain for a field, a farm, a peasant or a shepherd. Gaming is its serious affair, and its serious affairs have the air of a game. Its sovereign prince, the last absolute monarch, invested with divine right, ruling over a country of which from the top of his fortress-palace he can see the whole extent, disposes of the powers of a Genghis-Khan in order to retain for his subjects the privilege of not paying him any taxes. All things considered, nothing is so restful as a certain peaceful-looking absurdity. The words which I heard one of the many gardeners of Monte Carlo say, by way of urging on one of his fellows: "We must hurry up and water, it's going to rain," did not seem to me extravagant in the place where they were uttered.

Colette had ended by finding in Monte Carlo that masterpiece of artifice—a real set-piece—a "paper-weight" charm. It was the same with the Hôtel de Paris with its dining-room almost collapsing under the weight of its gold and bad paintings, its hall where overburdened multi-millionaires and exotic, be-diamonded highnesses sit in rows. There, very ancient old people take up their abode, awaiting over the years the hour when they will obtain access to a palace on the far side of the grave, a paradise *de luxe*.

Colette dreaded the visits of unknown people because she knew that at such times she was in the limelight and that embarrassed her. But she did not dislike mingling with the crowd since she kept the illusion that there she would pass unnoticed. As the majority of the hotel clients were foreigners, she thought all the more that they would not know who she was, and so she was therefore quite ready to go to the bar or the hall or the dining-room. It will be remembered what tributes were paid to her on her eightieth birthday. We left for Monte Carlo soon afterward. The first time that, pushing her wheel-chair, I took her into the hall at the hotel, the people who were there spontaneously rose and

bowed. Forgetting once again who she was and that her portrait had just appeared in all the newspapers of the world,
Colette turned to me eyes full of astonishment and innocence: "Oh! Maurice," she said, "d'you see? They remember
me from last year!"

The hotel staff were full of attentions for her. At the
bar there was always waiting for her a drink which, under
the tempting English name of barley water, was nothing but
syrup of orgeat, and a bunch of radishes which the head bar-
man, Monsieur Victor, obtained for her in all seasons. The
news agent, the cloakroom attendant were entitled to a
little visit, and then we went to lunch. In the afternoon,
even on holiday, Colette worked or wrote letters, for the
act of writing had become necessary to her; the habit of it
was too old to die.

Thus she was able in turn to satisfy her need of rest and
solitude, and to mingle with her fellows if she wanted to; her
life in Paris forbade both.

It was during our second stay at Monte Carlo, in the spring
of 1951, that Colette showed she had lost none of her keen-
ness of sight. The American play which Anita Loos had
adapted from *Gigi* was to appear on Broadway in the autumn. Anita Loos and the producer of the play, Gilbert
Miller, were searching America and England for a young
actress for the part of Gigi. This is a choice which will always be difficult, since it means finding a very young actress
with enough natural gifts to make up for an experience
which she cannot help lacking. But there is no part better
adapted for a dazzling revelation.

In Monte Carlo itself at that time a film called *Rendez-*

*Vous à Monte Carlo* was being made. The film people had
got permission to shoot some scenes in the hall of the Hotel
de Paris. On that particular day they had promised to leave
by noon. At one o'clock they were still shooting. When I
arrived, pushing Colette in her little chromium chair, we
stumbled over cables and projectors. We stopped to gaze at
a charming and very young English girl, who, under the
light of the projectors, was struggling half in English and
half in French. Hardly had Colette watched her perform for
a moment than she turned to me and said: "There is our
Gigi for America. Don't let's look anywhere else."

"All right," I answered, "I'll try and arrange it."

I saw the young actress that same afternoon. She bore the
unknown name of Audrey Hepburn, lived in London, had
by chance obtained this tiny part that needed an English
accent, danced and had never played in the theatre. When
I asked her whether she would be prepared if the chance
offered to go to New York to create the role of Gigi there,
she raised to heaven eyes that have since become famous
on the screen. I wrote at once to Anita Loos advising her
not to engage anyone before seeing the girl whom Colette
had chosen.

I do not know whether the stars of the cinema will for
posterity become shooting stars, or whether there will be a
Kean, a Talma, a Mademoiselle Mars of the screen. I am not
sure, because of the constant change in techniques, whether
the preservation of their films will be the best way of per-
petuating the fame of the stars. The prestige of Sarah Bern-
hardt, as far as the young are concerned, seems to me more
compromised than helped by the records which we have of

her. People will object that it is not yet like that for Chaplin or Raimu. The future will tell.

But what will be remembered is that, when she was seventy-eight, Colette, with a mere glance and a word, made a star rise in the theatrical firmament.

# XXVI

OUR STAY at Monte Carlo in the first two years took place in the spring and went on until the beginning of July. So as not to spend August in Paris I took Colette to the Hotel Trianon at Versailles. Later we preferred to spend the winter in the south, returning to Paris for Easter. From then on Colette dreaded the heat. Because of its cool climate, I chose Deauville two summers running. The crowd which gathers there did not seem to me a major inconvenience, since its sauntering is less congested there than elsewhere and experience has proved to me that from that point of view it is better to walk into the lion's den than to linger near it.

Colette was happy at Deauville, as long as she could circulate in her wheel-chair there. She went to performances of ballet and to the cinema, she was seen on the esplanade by the shore, nearly always in good spirits. But occasionally she was overcome by long periods of fatigue. And when the time came to return to the Palais-Royal she did so without regret.

It was there that her true place was, it was there that she

gathered around her her last symbols and consulted her familiar oracles. It is time that I took you into her room.

The flat is deep and narrow. In one side it gives on to the Rue Vivienne and on the other, through three windows, on to the garden of the Palais-Royal. Two of these windows belong to the main room, which is prolonged by a bedroom, less wide, which is lit only by the first room. This for a long time was Colette's own domain and she would put her divan-bed sometimes in the bedroom and sometimes in what she called the "living-room," * finally ending up with it along-side one of the two windows. The third room was that of my bedroom, which leads to a bathroom.

When Colette began to have difficulty in getting about, even at home, I persuaded her to install herself in my bedroom, which was smaller, more intimate, warmer in winter and nearer to the bathroom. It was entirely hung with a red paper, self-coloured and shiny, with white plinths and doors. Red is my favourite colour. Colette's used to be blue, but I had little by little drawn her in my direction, not indeed by persuasion but rather as a result of sympathy. She had even ended by going one better than I and soon everything in her room was red: curtains, armchair and bed.

She always covered her walls with paper and her ceilings with the same paper as the walls. She declared that a ceiling is a wall like any other, that man is not made to sit but to stand or lie, that he ought to spend his life as much lying down as standing, and so why inflict on his sight a great white surface which only drives him back on himself?

This bedroom became indeed her bedroom. Nothing will be changed in it as long as that depends on me, and I ex-

---

* *La pièce à vivre,* an unusual expression in French.

press the wish that it should be kept thus, so well does it reflect the Colette of those last years, her vagabondage at anchor and her power of creating the marvellous with everyday objects.

When one is looking at the Palais-Royal, this bedroom is to the right of the "living-room," and its window occupies the extreme right. So Colette's divan-bed was pushed with its foot against the wall, leaving only a narrow passage between itself and the window. Behind her there was a double door covered by a sliding curtain of thick red satin. In front of her, filling almost the whole panel between the window and the chimney-piece, which divides the room more or less in two, there is an arcaded niche hollowed out of the wall and containing three shelves on to which were crowded the books she most often read. Little by little these books became masked by the boxes of multi-coloured butterflies, by the transparent skeletons of shells, by ornaments full of emblematic meanings. It was quite a feat to reach the books without upsetting anything.

From the window Colette used to look out through the balustrades which run the length of the first and fourth stories of the uniform houses which, on three sides, encircle "the imprisoned garden," while the Palais itself closes the rectangle. The windows have panels filled in up to breast height; and as the Palais-Royal is classified as an historic monument and subject to strict conditions, we had to obtain from the Beaux-Arts permission to replace the panels in Colette's room by windows. If Monsieur Ventre had still been the responsible architect of it would he have permitted this? Colette speaks in *Trois . . . Six . . . Neuf . . .* of this astonishing personage who, from his balcony in the Rue de

Valois, used to inspect with naval binoculars the façades of the Palais-Royal, in the hope of surprising those who were infringing the regulations which he himself was continually contravening. An old man of redoubtable strength, with a fiery eye and a satanic beard, he would pummel you while he was speaking to you with blows of his fist which left you black and blue. Apart from that he spent his leisure in designing plans for state funerals, not so much for personalities who appeared to deserve them as for those whom he liked. It was his way of showing you friendship.

But from the time of Chodruc-Duclos, and so many others, the Palais-Royal has always welcomed extravagance without appearing to be aware of it. It finds it quite natural that a big green macaw "which resembled Offenbach" should be called Anatole, that it should go for a walk in company with a tortoise called Julie, that one should go and borrow from the Bank of France the ladder that is kept for burying gold, in order to help a cat overcome with dizziness at the top of a tree. It shows its familiarity with the great institutions which surround it: the Banque de France, the Conseil d'Etat, the Comédie-Française, the Bibliothèque Nationale. Colette herself did not hesitate to mobilize the whole of the Bibliothèque Nationale to find for her an illustrated work on Scottish Tartans with their exact colours, for an embroidery design. It is true that the Bibliothèque Nationale asked her in exchange for an inscription—*tu quoque, fili*—which will be found at the beginning of *La Treille Muscate* illustrated by Dunoyer de Segonzac: "To my great and glorious neighbour the Bibliothèque Nationale which lends me its shadow and sounds for me the hours of the day and the night. . . ."

When the Palais-Royal still had its prostitutes, it eyed them reprovingly. For all that, when the one who was called "the Countess," because she was one, and who continued to ply her trade at eighty, fell ill, the Palais-Royal got up a subscription so that she could be looked after. Colette had struck up an acquaintance with one of them, of whom she speaks in *L'Etoile Vesper* under the name of Renée, from the Cher. She had a face without any expression; she always greeted Colette in the same way: "Let me tell you, Madame Colette," and confided in her in the most artless way, talking of things to do with her job as though it were a question of selling a piece of trimming. All the same she had principles, albeit unexpected ones, and she was secretly bringing up a young brother on the proceeds of the tariff for her surrenderings. She wrote Colette letters that were poetic in their innocence and asked one day for a gift of one of her books.

"Which one?" asked Colette.

"The saddest," she answered.

In between two recommendations for a Legion of Honour, which Colette made to the Ministers concerned, she intervened on the subject of Madame Renée's professional registration card, which was not in order. Renée loved flowers so much that she finally decided to retire from the business of gallantry to take a stand at the Halles. Once again it was Colette who obtained it for her. By way of thanking her, Renée sometimes came early in the morning to offer Colette flowers still dripping with dew. I think she is there still.

The Palais-Royal and Colette were born to understand each other and a perfect connivance had established itself between them. Its natives approached Colette with that mixture of respect and niceness which is compounded in the heart. They kept away the tactless from her, and those who did not "belong." In return, Colette's door was never closed for Mademoiselle Mauduit, who sold lampshades and canvas for tapestry, for Rose Cohen, the little antique-dealer, for Madame Groves, the book-seller, for Madame Albert, for the baker's children or those of the concierge next door. When they passed through the garden they waved to her and from her window she replied with ample gestures.

And then Raymond Oliver, three houses away from us, bought the Restaurant Véfour which, by a miracle, has kept intact its ravishing interior dating from the end of the eighteenth century. We had always known the Véfour, half asleep, more of a café than a restaurant, given over to chess players and unambitious cooking. An attempt by a great Parisian restaurant-keeper to bring it out of its torpor had not succeeded. The Palais-Royal had rather looked askance at this innovator, although he did inhabit one side of its rectangle. How would it receive Raymond Oliver, a pure-bred Girondin, who came up from Langon where his family keeps a famous gastronomic posting house, in order to conquer Paris?

Raymond Oliver installed himself with calm assurance in the traditionalism of the Palais-Royal. Perhaps the best way of conquering a domain is to consider it as conquered. Naturally imposing, with sweeping gestures, endowed with a powerful voice, with the flow of speech and the irrepressible accent which characterise the man of the Southwest, in the twinkling of an eye Oliver had got the district in his pocket, including its most celebrated representatives. Even before they had noticed what was happening to them, Colette had composed a brochure for the launching of the new restaurant, while Christian Bérard had done a drawing and Cocteau an article.

The Véfour became our meeting-place. Our friends invited us there, and we received them there. Two waiters in the restaurant, in their white coats, would go and collect Colette in her sedan-chair, and walk all down the Rue de Beaujolais with her in this contraption. The Palais-Royal watched this procession pass with tender looks, withering with their glances any loiterers who dared to be surprised by it.

One summer day in 1951, when we had hardly finished lunch at home—Colette, her daughter and I—by chance I looked into the garden and noticed our concierge walking his little four-year-old boy. Suddenly I saw him look up, seize his son under his arm and begin to run. Other people stopped, open-mouthed, and I realised that there was a fire on the mezzanine floor, exactly below us. I hurried to find Pauline and said to her: "Put Madame in the sedan-chair. There's a fire downstairs. We'll take her down."

So as not to cause panic I had said that in my most ordinary voice. It was precisely what I ought not to have done. It is better to do violence to one's nature. There is a certain expression of alarm which suits such circumstances, and without it one fails to make oneself understood. I rapidly put into a little suitcase some precious manuscripts and books, just as people do in novels. When I went into Colette's room, nothing had been done: Pauline had not been able to get into her head, with my unconcerned air, that the house really was on fire. By the time we had unfolded the chair and got Colette into it, it was too late. The staircase was full of smoke which we could not have got through; we were in a trap.

We lived through some dramatic moments. The fire had started in the mezzanine floor while it was empty and had been smouldering for some time. Now it was roaring briskly. Those old houses of the Palais-Royal are full of dry wood which age has made very brittle. If the fire reached the floors, the whole house would have gone up like a torch.

Just before the smoke became impassable, Raymond Oliver had come up to our flat to lend a hand and help get Colette down. He seemed to think that quite natural, but I did not. It is one thing to put up calmly with what you cannot avoid, and another to go through smoke in order to shut yourself up with people who are in the position of herrings on a grill. Flamboyant speech, bordering on bombast, does not always go hand in hand with courageous acts, soberly carried out. That day Raymond Oliver acquired my undivided esteem and friendship.

Meanwhile a crowd had gathered in the garden. They could see the flames clearly. In that habitual compassionate language that such strong emotions call forth, they cried to us:

"Jump, you poor things, we can see your floors giving way!"

None of us moved, since in any case it was impossible to make Colette perform acrobatics. Perfectly aware of the danger, she remained calm. We suddenly heard her say: "All the same, there's no reason why we shouldn't have our coffee."

With that we were all agreed.

As soon as the firemen arrived, everything went very

quickly. There was a great breaking of windows and in a twinkling the fire was extinguished. But after all, the roads leading to the Palais-Royal are narrow. If a bottle-neck had occurred! It was a question of minutes.

# XXVII

EVERYTHING WAS perfectly organised on the "raft" for the thenceforward motionless voyage, in time and space, work on board, and soon, alas! the ship-wreck. A table into which had been incorporated a desk with an adjustable rack was an essential part of it. It straddled the bed without touching its sides. Made of mahogany, English in style and about half a yard wide, it was supported by two little columns on each side, and by feet which, though solid, were made to slide easily. Sitting on her divan, her back supported by a quantity of cushions, among which some trapezoidal ones came to her from America, Colette had always under her hand two sticks with crooked handles. With extreme dexterity she used them like hooks to get hold of the table at the end of her bed, a book or an object which seemed out of reach.

"You see," she said to me, "I go fishing, too, on the raft!"

On the table-desk there was, first of all, in a little porcelain pot of azure-blue verging on China-blue, the "bunch of fountain-pens," six or seven dumpy fountain-pens, each of which had its role: one was kept for correspondence, an-

other "knew how to correct proofs," a third preferred novels.
Alongside the "fountain-pen pot" lay "the all-purpose knife
and its scorpion tail," an elegant Spanish knife with a handle of chased-silver, whose ornamented blade had fortunately
lost its cutting edge. It did, indeed, serve every purpose,
among others that of opening the watches with which Colette surrounded herself. She had a craze for "examining
their stomachs," which led them fairly often to the watch-
repairers. A few months before her death the all-purpose
knife disappeared, the old servitor deserted: all efforts to
find it were vain.

A case for a book, in the form of a box of brown morocco,
used to intrigue the visitor, who could read, printed in gold
letters between the ribs of the case, the title of its contents:
*Pascal, Les Provinciales.* Who would have thought that this
was Colette's favourite reading? After a moment, Colette
would open the box and take out of it a little mirror, a lip-
stick or some other coquettish accessory. This case had en-
closed a very precious little volume which I brought back
to the house one day, clasping it to my heart. I could never
interest Colette in bibliophily: her relations with books
were different. She paid very little attention to the delicate
marvel, but immediately saw the use that could be made of
the case. I gladly let her have it.

A black blotting-pad with green blotting-paper, scissors,
a paper-knife, a spectacle case, the telephone, a little red
leather document-case, and one or two files completed the
permanent instruments of her work. The rest depended on
leisure or whim: a book of travels, an album of flowers,
paper-weights, exotic seeds, rare shells, photographs, compasses, a handyman's tool-kit.

Hooked on to the wall, just above Colette's head, was the barometer. Hanging on one of the balustrades, within seeing distance, the thermometer. She had at every moment to be able to diagnose and forecast the weather. And finally the blue lantern, the star-board light, although according to the way she was facing, it was on the left: it was a draughtsman's lamp, fixed to the wall, and whose arm could be bent in every direction. It had a daylight-coloured bulb in it, that is to say bluish, but what gave it its name was the shade which Colette made for it out of two sheets of the blue paper she used for her work; she had never found anything which served its purpose better.

Two contrary movements marked the last years of her life. The flow of fame which, swelling unceasingly, making its most resounding trumpets sound in her ears, multiplying honours for her, bringing to her table a pile of messages, and to her door a flood of visitors, reached a summit rarely surpassed. And the slow ebb of Colette herself, who attempted to escape from the noise created around her, not from any disdain that she might have of it, but because, feeling her powers diminishing and incapable of giving things a less wondering attention, she fell back upon what was essential for her, on what she was still able to clasp to her heart.

In winter, however well warmed the flat was, a wood fire crackled in Colette's chimney. Even when young, she felt the cold. She always had a shawl over her shoulders, and under the fur bedspread a hot-water bottle warmed her feet. Throughout the flat there was a rug under every cushion. When we had friends to lunch or dinner they found scarves and rugs on their chairs and finally gave in to Colette who insisted that one must keep warm while eating, so that soon we looked like a collection of Russian troika drivers. The little dining-room, which had many uses, was a room cut out of a courtyard, lighted from above and rather like an aquarium. Sometimes we received there the great ones of this world who, around our round table and on unmatching plates, enjoyed their share of Pauline's peasant cooking: the leg of lamb and the roast chicken served in the dish in which they had been cooked and carved by Colette, the *boeuf à la mode* and the country stew. Queen Elizabeth of Belgium was not differently treated and seemed enchanted by it.

No visit gave Colette greater pleasure than that one. The Queen climbed our steep steps, her arms laden with flowers, and with honey from her own bees, would not even let me relieve her of these on entering, and sat down at the foot of Colette's bed. There was no resisting her smile, her exquisite simplicity, her true humanity. One day, just as she was taking leave of Colette, she said to her that she would like to give her a present and begged her to guide her choice. If I had been in Colette's place I might perhaps have been tempted to mention a little Van Eyck in the Museum at Antwerp, or a tapestry from Bruges. Colette asked for some kriek-lambik. She had to give the Queen some explanations. Kriek-lambik, is, in fact, a very alcoholic beer made with cherries, and only sold in the lowest bars in Belgium. I don't know in what slums of Brussels they were found, but a few days later the embassy car solemnly brought us six bottles of this unspeakable beverage.

I passed all my evenings at home with her. At nightfall they close the gates which give access to the garden of the Palais-Royal and there is then no more silent place. The tall red velvet curtains of the window were drawn. Under the blue lantern Colette read a book of travels, setting off with an ill-equipped nineteenth century traveller for a *terra ignota*. Intoxicated by history, I travelled in the past. The hours slipped by, harmonious and delicious. Silence is a touch-stone between couples. It needs very deep feeling before two people in the same room can absorb themselves in work or reading, the presence of the one not only not embarrassing the other but even supporting him, while between one and the other a current of tenderness and trust continues to be obscurely felt. But if we began to talk there was no end to our exchange. From Colette to me there came words of devotion and gratitude which left me confused, and which I only mention here to show the strength of her attachments and, at a time when the whole world was bowing before her, her humility. I answered her that it was she who had given me everything, including the chance of devoting to her that fervour which with so many men remains unused.

"Oh, how sorry I am for you," she used sometimes to say to me, "having a wife so much older than yourself."

I pointed out to her that if our difference in age had been the other way round, I should then be ninety-five years old, that I should have been dead long since, and that in dying I should never have been able to get over having to leave her. Is it fair that in the majority of cases it should be the more defenceless who remains alone? For Colette and me our disparity of age, such as it was, always worked in favour of our understanding and not against it.

We only spoke of death for practical purposes, or in a jesting way.

"Do you think that I'm going to die soon?"

I only had to answer: "Not before I've given you permission to do so," to bring a smile to her lips.

But all she wanted was to reckon the time that she had left to live. Neither she nor I understood anything of those terrors which man creates for himself concerning his death. In that belief in survival which he has worked out for himself, we never knew which to wonder at more, his arrogance or his faint-heartedness. And in addition, it seemed to us crazy that he should have attributed this privilege to himself. For Colette, it would have meant admitting a fundamental difference between animals and men, which she saw no reason to believe, nor that such a difference would necessarily be in man's power.

The richly coloured butterflies which bounded her immediate horizon came from the Amazon and had been offered her by a Madame Fourner, who possessed forty-five thousand of them. On each side of the recess with the white background where the books lodged, a narrow strip of wood had enabled her to hang, in its contemporary frame, a little portrait of Sido at eighteen, that miniature of Sophie Landoy, miraculously discovered in the *Marché aux Puces,* on the back of which can still be read to-day: *"My children, do not forget your worthy and virtuous mother";* other boxes of butterflies, a drawing by Louise Hervieu representing flies, a luminous enamel of a bunch of flowers on a burning blue background by Jean Serrières and a little painting of flowers by Katia Barjansky, painter and sculptor and a former friend of the days in Rome in 1917.

We had had to find a place for the television, last contact with actuality, at the expense of the books. Among the

books there were works on Paris. The favourite was called
*Promenades Dans Toutes Les Rues de Paris,* by the Marquis
de Rochegude, twenty-one charming little cardboard-bound
volumes in which Colette, when she could no longer go out,
wandered for hours at a time. The blue lantern did not disdain to illuminate the *bateaux-mouche.*

The fireplace was within Colette's field of vision. Its
chimney-piece was covered, jammed, with paper-weights and
sulphides, which sparkled under the lights like a multi-
coloured tablecloth and were reflected in the looking-glass.
These things had not been brought together in any spirit of
collection. Colette loved them and bought them before anyone else, as well as those sealed bottles which come from
Notre-Dame-de-Liesse in the Aisne, filled with water on
which float, on the principle of marine mines, dozens of
little votive figures. On another chimney-piece in the flat
were those Chinese crystal balls which satisfied Colette's
two-fold taste for the limpidity of springs, and for circles.
Glass walking-sticks, trumpets, pipes, and necklaces were
hung and lodged all over the place.

On the walls of Colette's bedroom there were a number
of little oil paintings, most of which came from the painters
who were friends and who, knowing her preferences, offered
her flowers and fruit. The only portrait to escape Colette's
ban on any representation of the human face was one of a
young woman by Marie Laurencin, because of its vague and
cloudy appearance.

A long life with its attachments, its infatuations, and its
passionate preferences had deposited there its fetishes, its
symbols, and its instruments, turning a bedroom somewhere
in the world into a place enchanted above all others.

France promoted her to the highest rank that any woman
has attained in the Legion of Honour, the insignia of Grand
Officier being handed to her by the Ministre de l'Education
Nationale in the course of a banquet. The City of Paris gave
her its Gold Medal; the ambassador of the United States
came up to the flat to bring her the Diploma of the National
Institute of Arts and Letters; she would have had the Nobel
Prize if she had been able to wait for it. She bore as well as
she could this burden of honours, standing up to it valiantly.
All movement was thenceforward forbidden to her, except
that of hoisting herself by the strength of her arms from her
divan to her little chromium chair, whose wheels she could
then manipulate. Her writing, which had remained so firm,
gradually changed, betraying the fatigue which she strove
to hide. Her memory detached itself from recent events so
that it might better hold the deeply graven traces of the
past. Two months before her end she found again a photograph taken in her school at Saint Sauveur, which shows
her among thirty little girls aged from eight to twelve; she
named them all, one after the other, without hesitation.

Our departure for Monte Carlo was delayed by the rehearsals of the French play *Gigi,* at which I felt I must be
present. They begged me to let Colette go to the first night
of *Gigi,* but I remembered her most recent appearances in
public, at the first night of *Chéri* and that of *La Seconde.* I
was the last person to wish to put a brake on the enthusiasm which made the whole audience rush towards her box.
follow her on the pavements and surround her car. But I
knew that glory had become for her too strong a drink.

For the first night of *Gigi,* fixed for February 24, the

French Television organised in "duplex" a conversation between Colette, who would not have to budge from home,
and her colleagues of the Académie Goncourt, who were
gathered in the Théatre des Arts. The evening wore on. I
was waiting by Colette until her turn to take part arrived.
She was extremely tired. All the same she improvised a few
phrases about love and youth, whose accent was all the more
moving for the weariness apparent in it.

We left Paris the next day. At home in winter Colette no
longer quitted her overheated bedroom. I hoped that in the
south with all the windows open, she would regain some
strength. For never at any moment or in any way was she ill.
All that happened was an imperceptible drooping.

We returned at the beginning of May.

Little by little she became more silent. Twice more she
went out in the car. She bent forward so as to see better.
The few people who were near her then will remember how
she held her two hands before her, at shoulder level, palms
forward, in a gesture of wonder. But she returned tired out.

It was towards the end of June that that lowering vitality,
that slow withdrawal, became marked. I noticed that she no
longer touched the newspapers which were brought to her
in the morning and hardly opened her letters. The exterior
world was receding too far away. She began to sleep a great
deal. When she awoke from those deep sleeps, she would
first lift to her ear a big repeater-watch which struck the
hours, the quarters and the minutes in a silvery voice. Then
she consulted the weather, the position of the sun, and got
her bearings on the raft. She took an interest in fewer
things, but not less in those. She rang for Pauline, asked her
for a book of pictures representing plants, birds and insects.

Nearly always now she used a magnifying glass, not because her sight had diminished but because she wanted to look more closely. And she asked to see her butterflies nearer.

Then came the day when she was too weak to raise herself. It was towards the twentieth of July. Colette de Jouvenel, Pauline and I started a vigil whose duration we could not guess, although we knew how it must end.

A nurse helped Pauline. What Pauline had hitherto done alone surpassed human strength. She carried Colette, heavy though she was, into her bath and pulled her out of it, served her all day, got up three times in the night, and remained on the alert at her door. Their understanding came from afar, and had its roots in the earth. But more recently Pauline had become the indispensable arm, the arm one gropes for in the half-shadows. Only to Pauline could the weariness, the weakness, the failing be admitted, only to her a face unadorned be shown.

From all those last days we have kept nothing but images of sweetness. Colette only came out of her long torpors to give tender looks and angelic smiles addressed in turn to her daughter, to Pauline and to me. We sat her up and she asked for her butterflies, her illustrated books, raising in the air her little hands which mysteriously had become younger. Her face took on a strange beauty.

Or else I would watch her sleeping, and the feeling which governed me was that of gratitude. For thirty years of unclouded happiness she had enabled me to live in an enchanted world, and offered me a picture of such greatness that I despair of being able to bear witness to it, though at least I shall have tried. She did me the favour of going out without suffering, like a sun which sinks, at peace with her-

self and with all that surrounded her. She fulfilled in every
way the wish that she herself had many years before expressed:

"And when you lie down across the dizzying, wavy path,
if you have not already shed your curly locks one by one,
nor one by one your teeth, if your limbs have not worn out
one by one, if the dust of the world has not, before your last
hour, sealed your eyes from the marvellous light, if you
have, right to the end, kept in your hand the friendly hand
which guides you, lie down smiling, sleep happily, and sleep
privileged. . . ."

All was well for her, all was ended for the two of us, since
everything has to end. I even consider that it was just that
I should remain behind and take upon myself the burden
of living, the pain of surviving.

I went out one morning to find a book for her and brought
her back a beautiful album of coloured lithographs representing butterflies, insects and birds, which enchanted her.
She read the descriptions aloud, following them with her
finger. One of the butterflies was called *blaps, portent of
death*.

Two days before the end, she emerged from a great weariness into an hour of great lucidity. We looked at the album
together. I was sitting on the floor in the space between the
bed and the window. It was a hot August day with a veiled
sky. The swallows were passing level with the open window,
with sharp whirrings. Colette bent toward me and I put my
head against her side. She pointed to the boxes of butterflies on their shelf, the book, and the birds in the garden.
"Ah!" she said. So near to death and knowing it, everything

appeared to her more beautiful and more wonderful than ever. Her hands fluttered about her like wings. She leaned a bit closer to me. Her arm described a spiral which embraced everything that she had shown me: "Look!" she said to me, "Maurice, look!"

She spoke no more after that.

But the next day she came again out of her somnolence with a radiant visage. With half-closed eyes she pronounced, in mute syllables, very distinctly, a veritable discourse which was no longer addressed to any of us. She appeared intensely happy. Her hands remained raised in the air when all strength had already abandoned her.

As far as I could guess, flattering myself that communication between her and me continued right up to the last moment, she was back in the garden of her childhood: she was speaking to Sido, to Sido found again at last. "To reach completion is to return to one's starting point." She had returned to her starting point. "My instinctive bent which takes pleasure in curves and spheres and circles": the circle was closed, the curve led her back to those springs in her own country, of which she had hoped that it might be given her "at the moment when all must end" to take with her "an imaginary draught."

On August 3rd, toward half-past seven in the evening, not having been out for many days, I decided to go for an hour's walk. But I cut short my walk, finding no peace except at home. Pauline was standing beside Colette and I stayed to watch with her. Colette was asleep. It was very close, the sky was low and the Palais-Royal deserted. Colette's breathing became more raucous, and we looked at each other, Pauline and I. This lasted for about a quarter of an hour. We remained motionless. Suddenly there was silence and Colette's head bent slowly to one side, with a movement of infinite grace.